# ALL ABOUT GERANIUMS

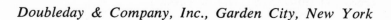

# ALL ABOUT
## GERANIUMS

*by Peggie Schulz*

DRAWINGS BY ISABEL JONES

*Doubleday & Company, Inc., Garden City, New York*

*To our daughters, Myrna, Gayle, and Katie*

# Contents

| | | |
|---|---|---|
| | Acknowledgments | *xi* |
| | Author's Memo | *xiii* |
| 1 | Geraniums: A Proud Past, an Exciting Future | *1* |
| 2 | Geranium Growing Guide | *10* |
| 3 | Potting, Pruning, and Propagating Geraniums | *20* |
| 4 | Hybridizing Geraniums | *30* |
| 5 | Geranium Diseases and Pests | *37* |
| 6 | Wintering Geraniums | *43* |
| 7 | Heading the Popularity Poll | *47* |
| 8 | Miniature, Dwarf, and Semidwarf Geraniums | *56* |
| 9 | Fancy-leaved Geraniums | *65* |
| 10 | Scented-leaved Geraniums | *73* |
| 11 | Trailing and Climbing Ivy-leaved Geraniums | *87* |
| 12 | Lady Washington Pelargoniums | *94* |
| 13 | Geraniums for Collectors | *103* |
| 14 | Growing Geraniums with Artificial Light | *117* |
| 15 | Geraniums in the Greenhouse | *124* |
| 16 | Geranium Trees and Other Trained Forms | *134* |
| 17 | Decorating with Geraniums | *140* |
| 18 | True Geraniums and Related Plants | *151* |
| 19 | Geranium Societies, Shows, Projects, and Programs | *160* |
| 20 | How and Where to Buy Seeds and Plants of Geraniums and Pelargoniums | *165* |
| | Index | *168* |

# List of Illustrations

## COLOR

*Between pages 48 and 49*

[1]. Geraniums blooming in home greenhouse
[2]. Zonal geraniums in window box with browallia
[3]. 'Dark Red Irene' geraniums in holiday-mood topiary
[4]. Tubbed zonal geraniums at entryway to garden
[5]. Pink zonal geraniums in urn at doorway
[6]. Zonal geraniums in garden with blue and white ageratum
[7]. Ivy-leaved geranium 'Charles Turner' in hanging basket

*Between pages 112 and 113*

[8]. Fancy-leaved geraniums with typical blossoms
[9]–[20]. Twelve 'Lady Washington' geraniums

## BLACK AND WHITE

| | |
|---|---:|
| *Pelargonium hortorum* 'Tiny Tim,' miniature | 2 |
| Geranium collection on terrace in summer | 5 |
| Author's window garden of geraniums in winter | 6 |
| Geraniums on terrace by the seashore | 7 |
| Geranium 'Nittany Lion' from seed | 8 |
| Geraniums inside sun porch in winter with lobelia | 13 |
| Potted and tubbed geraniums with marguerites | 15 |
| Repotting rootbound geranium | 21 |
| Adding new soil at repotting time | 21 |
| Settling new soil around the roots | 21 |
| Eight-year-old pillar type zonal geranium | 23 |
| Taking a geranium cutting with sharp knife | 26 |
| Removing lower leaves and stipules from cutting | 26 |
| Dipping base of cutting in root-inducing hormone | 26 |
| Inserting cutting in moist sand for rooting | 26 |
| Three steps in grafting zonal geranium | 29 |

Preparing flat for sowing geranium seeds                       34
Adding half-inch layer of vermiculite                          34
Marking rows in vermiculite                                    35
Rubbing husks from seeds to aid germination                    35
Transplanting seeds with set of true leaves                    35
Floradale Fancy Mixed zonal geranium                           36
*Pelargonium hortorum* 'Fiat Queen'                            49
*Pelargonium hortorum* 'Pink Cloud'                            49
*Pelargonium hortorum* 'Princess Fiat'                         49
*Pelargonium hortorum* 'Apple Blossom'                         51
*Pelargonium hortorum* 'Honeymoon'                             51
*Pelargonium hortorum* 'Natalie Webster'                       51
*Pelargonium hortorum* 'Wicked Lady'                           52
*Pelargonium hortorum* 'Doc'                                   58
*Pelargonium hortorum* 'Emma Hossler' and 'Mr. Everaarts'      59
*Pelargonium hortorum* 'Fairy Tales'                           59
*Pelargonium hortorum* 'Fleurette'                             59
*Pelargonium hortorum* 'Kleiner Liebling Variegated'           61
*Pelargonium hortorum* 'Red Spider'                            61
*Pelargonium hortorum* 'Rosy Dawn'                             61
*Pelargonium hortorum* 'Sneezy'                                62
*Pelargonium hortorum* 'Snow White'                            62
*Pelargonium hortorum* 'Tinkerbelle'                           62
*Pelargonium hortorum* 'Trinket'                               62
*Pelargonium hortorum* 'Alpha'                                 66
*Pelargonium hortorum* 'Verona'                                66
*Pelargonium hortorum* 'Skies of Italy' and
  'Pink Happy Thought'                                         66
*Pelargonium hortorum* 'Pollock 137,' 'Jubilee,' and
  'Miss Burdett Coutts'                                        67
*Pelargonium hortorum* 'Wilhelm Langguth'                      67
*Pelargonium hortorum* 'Miss Burdett Coutts'                   67
Scented-leaved Geranium 'Red-flowered Rose'                    76
Scented-leaved Geranium 'Little Gem'                           76
Scented-leaved Geranium 'Mint-scented Rose'                    76
Scented-leaved Geranium 'Grey Lady Plymouth'                   77
Scented-leaved Geranium 'Snowflake'                            77
Scented-leaved Geraniums 'Shrubland Rose,' 'Fair Ellen,'
  and 'Little Gem'                                             78
Scented-leaved Geranium 'Apple'                                78
Scented-leaved Geranium 'Mrs. Kingsley'                        79
Scented-leaved Geranium 'Scarlet Unique'                       80
Scented-leaved Geranium 'Prince of Orange'                     80

Scented-leaved Geranium 'Crispum Minor'                     81
Scented-leaved Geranium Grape Leaf                          83
Topiary Tree of Scented-leaved Geraniums                    84
How to make topiary tree                                   84
*Pelargonium peltatum* 'Sunset' ('L'Élégante')             88
*Pelargonium peltatum* 'Mexican Beauty'                    90
*Pelargonium peltatum* 'New Dawn'                          90
*Pelargonium peltatum* 'Santa Paula'                       90
Author's ivy-leaved geranium on cholla wood               92
Closeup showing roots of ivy-leaved geranium              92
Author's topiary of ivy-leaved geranium                   92
*Pelargonium domesticum* 'African Belle'                  95
*Pelargonium domesticum* 'Bimbo'                          95
*Pelargonium domesticum* 'Black Lace'                     95
*Pelargonium domesticum* 'Chicago Market'                 96
*Pelargonium domesticum* 'Chorus Girl'                    96
*Pelargonium domesticum* 'Dubonnet'                       96
*Pelargonium domesticum* 'Empress of Russia'              98
*Pelargonium domesticum* 'Grand Slam'                     98
*Pelargonium domesticum* 'Mrs. Layal'                    100
*Pelargonium domesticum* 'Waltz Time'                    101
Rosebud Geranium 'Apple Blossom'                          105
Cactus- or Poinsettia-flowered Geranium 'Noel'           106
'White Bird's-egg' Geranium                               107
'Mr. Wren' Geranium                                       108
*Pelargonium dasycaule*                                   109
*Pelargonium formosum*                                    110
*Pelargonium fulgidum*                                    111
*Pelargonium gibbosum*                                    112
*Pelargonium* x *rutaceum*                                113
*Pelargonium salmoneum*                                   114
*Pelargonium scandens*                                    114
*Pelargonium* x *Stapletonii*                             115
*Pelargonium tetragonum*                                  116
Geraniums growing in fluorescent-lighted bookcase         121
Geraniums in greenhouse at Merry Gardens                  125
Curved-eave aluminum home greenhouse                      126
Frankly fake geranium tree                                136
How to make frankly fake geranium tree                   136
Pseudo bonsai geranium: *Pelargonium divaricatum*        138
Pseudo bonsai geranium: *Pelargonium abrotanifolium*     139
Potted zonal geraniums in terra-cotta tubs               141
Collection of geraniums in apartment window              142

Zonal geraniums in planter with variegated *Vinca major*       143
Zonal geraniums used to decorate outdoor living area       144
Weathered log container for small geraniums       145
Easy arrangement of geraniums and chrysanthemums       147
Zonal geraniums arranged for holiday table       148
Zonal geraniums combined with redwood planter       149
Zonal geraniums in contemporary planting arrangement       150
*Geranium cinereum*       155

## LINE DRAWINGS

*(By Isabel Jones except as noted)*

Containers for Geraniums       18
How to Hybridize Geraniums       32
Verticillium Symptoms       38
Geranium Diseases       40
Ideas for Wintering Geraniums       44
Miniature Geraniums under Fluorescent Lights       46
True Geraniums from Some Old Herbals       153
Dove's-foot Cranesbill from an Old Herbal       154
Erodiums from an Old Herbal       158
The Rare Monsonia       159

# Acknowledgments

I could not write a gardening book without the help of specialists, hobbyists, and friendly correspondents who give freely of their gardening knowledge. To the many wonderful gardeners who have shared their geranium experiences with me, my heartfelt thanks. There is not space to list you by name here, but your few lines on a postcard and your letters filled with glowing reports of successes or lines saddened with small failures have helped to write this book.

I am grateful to the International Geranium Society for the use of its fine monthly publication, *Geraniums Around the World*.

My special thanks go to the professional geranium growers who answered my questions and helped in so many other ways. Mary Ellen Ross, of Merry Gardens, Camden, Maine, whose knowledge of geraniums and other plants is remarkable, always answered my letters quickly and supplied many of the photographs for this book. Fred Bode, Jr., Southern California Geranium Gardens, Escondido, California, counseled me wisely, and furnished valuable information about the most popular geranium varieties and trends in geranium breeding. Waldo L. Cook, Cook's Geranium Nursery, Lyons, Kansas, shared similar information with me. Robert Warner, Manhattan Garden Supply, Manhattan Beach, California, let me spend hours among his plants and patiently answered my questions personally and by mail.

These Minnesota professional growers shared plants and knowledge: Robert Anderson, Tonkadale Greenhouses, Hopkins; Bachman's, Minneapolis; Madsen's Floral Company, Minneapolis.

Clara and Harry May, Long Beach, California, invited me to visit them and see their marvelous collection of Pelargoniums (geraniums), including exquisite hybrid regals. They gave me color slides to help in identifying some of their newest varieties.

Robert Schweitze, Supervisor of Floriculture of Como Park Conservatory, St. Paul, Minnesota, accompanied me on note-taking tours through the geranium collection in the conservatory's magnificent greenhouses.

Thanks, also, to the men who allowed me to read reports of geranium projects undertaken by them or by their students: G. E. Beck, Associate Professor of Horticulture, University of Wisconsin, Madison, for Michael D. Paulsen's paper "Geranium Grafting"; Richard S. Lindstrom, Associate Professor of Horticulture, Michigan State University, East Lansing, for notes on the use of growth retardants and stimulators on geraniums, and a copy of "Gibberellin and Higher Plants: 1X Flowering in Geranium (*Pelargonium hortorum*)" by Professor Lindstrom and S. H. Wittwer; Professor A. Kivilaan, Department of Botany and Plant Pathology, Michigan State University, East Lansing, Michigan, for two papers on diseases in pelargoniums by Professor Kivilaan and R. P. Sheffer.

I received considerable assistance from these California geranium specialists: Holmes C. Miller, Los Altos; Edith and Everett Pratt, Vista; Schmidt Nursery, Palo Alto; Gerry's Geranium Garden, Artesia.

Sincere thanks to Wilson Brothers, Roachdale, Indiana, for their suggestions and information.

To George B. Park, George W. Park Seed Company, Greenwood, South Carolina, a thank-you for lending nineteenth-century copies of *Park's Floral Magazine*.

My special and deep appreciation goes to Elaine Cherry, editor, garden writer, and successful gardener for the meticulous way she polished my manuscript at a time when my own schedule did not permit this work. I am grateful also to garden writers George Abraham, Naples, New York, and Robert Waln, Drexel Hill, Pennsylvania, for assistance and encouragement.

And to my husband and family goes my deepening love for their unfailing patience during the months it took to write this book.

# Author's Memo

Dear Readers:

As a child, I knew well the true geraniums of Wisconsin woodlands. Those lovely lavender-rose wildlings gave me flowers for my own small garden and perfect "pressing material" for school projects.

My grandmother grew garden geraniums in big, black kettles and stone crocks. They grew as beautifully in those homely containers as they do in our own glazed pots and handsome tubs.

Even now the rich, fruity smell of apples recalls not only the barrels of them stored in the cellar of my childhood home, but the handsome, satin-leaved, apple-scented geranium. But when it's time to make apple jelly, I think of the leaves of another fragrant geranium, rose-scented *Pelargonium graveolens;* its leaves were placed at the bottom of the jar to give the jelly its piquant flavor.

In California, geraniums run riot over yards and hillsides. Geranium hedges of advanced age grow luxuriantly in parks and private gardens. Most of us who live in colder climates cannot grow our geraniums on such a grand scale, but we *can* grow them to perfection.

A few choice geranium specimens will add great appeal to your garden. Even cuttings exhibited beautifully on a gala "cutting tree" will make an effective display. Ivy-leaved trailing geraniums assume new importance when trained to rounded, topiary-tree forms or planted to cascade from a cholla wood trunk.

This book is for the gardener who is eager to know more about the many kinds of geraniums, who wants to discover new types to add to his collection, and who wants to enjoy growing geraniums.

Sincere effort has been made to report names correctly. I have used as references *The Dictionary of Gardening,* published by the Royal Horticultural Society; L. H. Bailey's *Standard Cyclopedia of Horticulture;* and an article, "Pelargoniums in Cultivation," by Harold E. Moore, Jr., published in *Baileya* (3:1:5 and 3:2:71), a publication of the Bailey Hortorium, Cornell University, Ithaca, New York.

May you have as much fun reading this book and working with your geraniums as I have in growing and writing about them.

Sincerely,

PEGGIE SCHULZ

Minneapolis, Minnesota
January 1964

# ALL ABOUT GERANIUMS

# 1

# *Geraniums:*
# *A Proud Past, an Exciting Future*

Geraniums are international favorites. They add color to window boxes, flower beds, and borders. School children take home small potted geraniums for Mother's Day gifts. Rows of bright-colored geraniums mingle with annuals and perennials at the garden shops in spring. Americans buy millions of these colorful plants every year. Geraniums are the sixth most important floral crop in the United States.

The most commonly-known geraniums are the cluster-flowered zonals (*Pelargonium hortorum*), with their everyday names of garden, bedding, or fish geraniums. But there are hundreds of others with beautiful flowers and exceptional foliage. In this remarkable family there are three-inch miniatures such as pink-flowered 'Tiny Tim'; ivy-leaved plants that spread to ten feet or more; fancy-leaved types with foliage of green-and-white, yellow-red-and-brown, or combinations of all these colors. There are gloriously perfumed scented-leaved geraniums with the rich odors of fruits, spices, roses, and peppermint. You will discover novelty plants like wiry-stemmed *Pelargonium reniforme* with furry leaves and rosy-purple flowers; and *P. tetragonum,* a pink-flowered climber with fleshy, jointed stems.

There are delightful double-flowering geraniums with blossoms like rosebuds; single-flowering plants with delicately spaced petals; and the gorgeous regal or show pelargoniums (popularly called Lady Washington, and sometimes Martha Washington, geraniums), with flowers like pansies or azaleas. The colors in the geranium

1. Pelargonium hortorum *'Tiny Tim' is a three-inch miniature with pink flowers.* PHOTO BY MERRY GARDENS

family range from pure white through shades of pink and red, to bronze and near-black.

Since the era of Pliny the Elder (A.D. 23–79), this fascinating group of plants has been traveling under the name *Geranium*. This is correct in a broad sense, because the plants belong to the Geranium Family, or the *Geraniaceae,* but strictly speaking they are of the genus *Pelargonium. Pelargonium* means "stork" and alludes to the resemblance of the seed case to the long, slender bill of the stork.

The word *Geranium,* from the classical Greek meaning "crane," expresses the similarity between the seed case and the bill of a crane. A third genus in the Geranium Family, *Erodium,* takes its name from a fancied or real resemblance of the seed case to the heron's bill.

The use of the name *Pelargonium* as a separate genus dates from 1789, and is attributed to the French botanist L'Héritier.

Pelargoniums have irregular flowers with the two upper petals often larger and more richly colored than the three lower petals. True geranium flowers are regular in form. The uppermost segment of a pelargonium's five-part calyx has at its base a narrow nectar-bearing tube or spur. A pelargonium has ten stamens, seven of which are tipped with pollen-bearing anthers. A geranium has ten pollen-bearing anthers, usually in two rows. Although many of the newer hybrids have more petals and fewer or more stamens than the classical forms, botanists and experienced plantsmen do not find it difficult to distinguish pelargoniums from the related hardy or wild (true) geraniums.

If you would like to see the pelargonium nectary, slice lengthwise through the pedicel or small stem of a pelargonium flower with a razor blade. Begin cutting directly at the base of the largest sepal (one of the five green parts of the calyx). You will see in the pedicel a small opening, or nectary tube. If you have some of the species pelargoniums in your collection, look closely at the pedicel and you will note a small angle or bend. This may be quite near the flower or it may be some distance away. The angle is the base of the nectary.

Most of us who grow the many wonderful kinds of pelargoniums will probably always call them geraniums, except the regals or Lady Washingtons which are commonly called pelargoniums or "pels." In this book I will follow the admonition "When thou art at Rome, do as they do at Rome"* and refer to the well-known garden varities, the ivy- and fancy-leaved types, and the collectors' choices, as "geraniums." When I mean the hardy or wild geraniums, I will speak of them as "true geraniums."


# CENTURIES OF ACCLAIM

If you enjoy doing research or studying old gardening books, you will have a field day with geraniums. Seventeenth-century traders carried species pelargoniums from South Africa to Holland and England. Dillenius, writing of James Sherard's garden at Eltham in

* Miguel de Cervantes, *Don Quixote*

1732, noted six species. Twenty-five species are described in Linnaeus' *Species Plantarum,* 1753. L'Héritier, who founded the genus *Pelargonium,* shows forty-four plates of pelargoniums in his work *Geraniologia de Brutelle,* which appeared in Paris in 1789.

Early nineteenth-century gardeners were excited about pelargoniums, but continued to call them geraniums. They hybridized the plants freely, particularly the regals. Hundreds of new forms were developed during the "geranium craze," which reached its peak between 1820 and 1830 with the publication of Robert Sweet's five-volume work, *Geraniaceae,* containing five hundred beautifully colored plants of pelargoniums and geraniums. Copies of *Geraniaceae* are rare today, but your public library may have them, or you may be able to see the books at a botanical garden library. I am fortunate to have access to the volumes at the Minneapolis Public Library as well as at the University of Minnesota's library. However, I warn you: do not think you are going to look at these books for just a few minutes. Be prepared to spend several hours or days reading and studying. You will be captivated by the descriptions and the colors in the beautifully executed drawings.

## GERANIUMS REDISCOVERED

Twentieth-century decorators and gardeners have rediscovered geraniums. We see them everywhere. A color page in a magazine shows a fashion designer decorating his penthouse balcony with red geraniums; the Four Seasons, an elite restaurant in New York City, displays hanging baskets of geraniums at the windows; a wallpaper firm uses geraniums to pattern one of its smartest papers; and a manufacturer creates elegant miniature topiary trees of geraniums.

Every spring, one of our largest department stores displays potted geraniums in all departments. Each pot is labeled, "Take me home . . . I'll brighten your garden." To help gardeners visualize how geraniums can vitalize a garden, the store plants window boxes with masses of glowing pink geraniums.

Geraniums are favorites in other countries, too. From Rome comes a picture showing a patio wall of colorful open tilework topped with ivy-leaved geraniums, and potted geraniums appear in lavish groupings all around the outdoor living area.

From Australia and England there are continuing reports of gera-

2. *A collection of geraniums benefits from a summer spent outdoors where there is protection from strong wind, rain, and sun, but where there is abundant fresh air. At the same time plants are summering outdoors, they can be arranged into handsome decorations for the outdoor living area, as this photograph shows.* PHOTO BY PAUL E. GENEREUX

3. *Author's window garden of geraniums in winter. Note pleasing display of flowers, even at a time when days are short.* PHOTO BY MEL JACOBSEN

niums used in arrangements and corsages, and of specimen plants winning top flower-show awards.

There has been a big upswing in the popularity of geraniums during the last decade. Magazines show beautiful illustrations of geraniums in container gardens, and infinite numbers of ways in which to use them decoratively as specimen plants, in flower beds, borders, baskets, and indoors. Standards, or tree geraniums, are requisites for stylish formal gardens, and they add a classic note to informal settings.

Gardeners challenged by the Oriental art of bonsai will find several kinds of geraniums which adapt perfectly to this exquisite gardening form. The miniature geranium 'Tiny Tim' is notable for bonsai work.

Flower arrangers will find unique possibilities in geraniums. The gardener who wants to make a bouquet or fashion a simple arrangement will discover that geraniums are made to order for easy-to-do designs.

With the sweeping expanses of glass in new classrooms, teachers are discovering that geraniums bring winter cheer indoors. While I was writing this book my small grandson, seeing geraniums all over our house, said, "I have the job of dusting under teacher's geraniums. I told her you let me help you with yours."

Geraniums are traffic stoppers in city beautification projects. I frequently visit one small Midwestern town which stages an annual

*4. Geraniums are the main floral decoration for this terrace by the seashore. They are used in window boxes, the basket is filled with an ivy-leaved variety, the rectangular bed is accented with four standard or tree geraniums, and there are zonals by the doorstep.* PHOTO BY PAUL E. GENEREUX

5. *'Nittany Lion' geranium is an outstanding strain to grow from seeds. Profuse flowering results within six months.*
PHOTO BY FERRY-MORSE SEED COMPANY

"Community Beautiful" campaign. Merchants place colorful plant-ings all around, area garden clubs sell the plants, then all help turn the planter boxes into a veritable flower land. The planters feature geraniums, petunias and variegated *Vinca major.* The effect is so colorful that people drive for miles to see this beautiful, flower-dec-orated town.

## FUTURE POSSIBILITIES

Walk through a greenhouse filled with geraniums, or turn the colorful geranium pages of flower catalogs, and you may wonder how these plants could possibly be improved. Yet, hybridizers always seek to develop better plants with a wider range of color, form and size. Many plant breeders have discovered species plants which add vigor to hybrid forms. One Western plantsman has predicted that some of these innovations will add totally new dimensions to the world of geraniums.

A California breeder is working on semidwarf regal geraniums. In Kansas, a hybridizer is breeding for flower-basket geraniums by crossing pink-flowered, dark-leaved *Pelargonium frutetorum* with fancy-leaved 'Dark Beauty,' 'Alpha,' and others, for he reports that he cannot keep enough stock of flower-basket varieties such as 'Black Lace' and 'Flower Basket.' And in New England, another grower reports that in the day-to-day operation of a commercial greenhouse, she continues to find mutations. Some of these are such outstanding departures from the originals that they are named and became permanent inhabitants of geranium collections the world over.

Personally, I hope to have someday a geranium with bright blue flowers, one with large clusters of lemon-yellow flowers, and others bred for fluorescent-light culture. I applaud the trend toward treating certain geranium strains as annuals, sowing the seeds in early spring for flowers that same year. While these and other advancements are made, it is my wish that more and more home gardeners will come to know and enjoy geraniums as I do.

# 2

## *Geranium Growing Guide*

Geraniums grow to their fullest beauty when they receive proper care. In time and with patience, each gardener learns to adjust his growing procedures to suit his own gardening conditions of light, temperature, humidity, soil, and water.

My basic suggestions are intended to get new growers off to a good start. Experienced gardeners who feel they are not getting a full quota of beauty from geraniums may profit, also. If you think that your geraniums might benefit from a change of soil or method of culture, use the new ideas on a few plants. If these methods give better results than your old ways, begin to apply them to your entire collection.

## THE GROWING MEDIUM IS IMPORTANT

The right soil is basic to the welfare of geraniums.

Soil should be friable (easily crumbled), drain quickly and well, and have a pH (acid-alkaline rating) of about 6.5. Soil-testing kits are available at most seed stores or from specialty houses. They are inexpensive and easy to use. Or, you can send a soil sample to your county agent or to the Department of Agriculture of your state university for testing.

Ready-to-use pasteurized geranium soil can be purchased from greenhouses, garden centers, and florists. This is a handy arrangement for new growers who wish to start with a few potted plants and for gardeners who lack storage space for soil.

Many growers purchase a mixture such as Black Magic, using it just as it comes from the package. Others stretch this commercial mixture by adding one-third sand or bird grit (available at bird and pet stores).

Consider first a simple soil formula (parts are by volume):

*3 parts garden soil*
*1 part peat moss or leaf mold*
*1 part sand*

(Peat moss is available locally from garden centers and from most hardware stores. Leaf mold is the term used to describe partially decayed leaves found in the forest or in a compost pile. Both ingredients can be purchased in small quantities from some of the houseplant specialists listed in Chapter 20.)

A container garden outdoors in an area where summers are hot and dry will benefit from a more moisture-retentive mixture such as this:

*3 parts garden soil*
*3 parts peat moss*
*1 part sand or perlite*

If your garden soil is poor, add a four-inch potful of a balanced fertilizer to a bushel of the above growing mix, or a teaspoonful to each five-inch pot.

An Eastern friend grows handsome geraniums in this soil mixture:

*1 bushel garden soil*
*⅓ bushel peat moss, leaf mold, compost, or well-rotted manure*
*⅓ bushel sand*
*1/12 bushel gritty material such as coal clinkers or perlite*
*1 four-inch potful of bone meal.*

One grower told me, "I never bother to mix special geranium soil. I just dig into the garden, get some soil and pot my plants in it." And you may, too, if your garden soil is friable and enriched. In a controlled experiment you might test your natural soil against a prepared mixture and compare the results.

Another gardener I know grows all her potted plants, including geraniums, in tin cans filled with sphagnum moss. Every watering includes a one-tenth strength solution of houseplant fertilizer.

## SOIL PASTEURIZATION

There are gardeners who grow gorgeous geraniums without pasteurizing or sterilizing the growing medium. But I play it safe and pasteurize all soil and other growing media used for cuttings and container-grown plants. Pasteurizing takes little time and kills harmful bacteria and soil-lodged pests. Pasteurize soil by heat or chemically.

Here is an easy way to accomplish the job by the heat method: Mix all components and place in two-pound coffee cans. Moisten with about one-half cup of water to a two-pound can of mix. Bake the mix for two hours in a 180-degree oven. Cans may be covered with lids or foil if desired. Remove the cans from the oven. Do not use the mix for twenty-four hours, and stir it thoroughly before using. If the mix is to be stored for future use, label the cans so you will know the type of mix and that it has been pasteurized.

If you prefer the chemical method, mix a tablespoonful of formaldehyde in a quart of water and sprinkle the solution over alternate layers of mix. Cover tightly and do not use the mix for seven to ten days.

I like to use insecticide capsules. I empty the soil mixture into a clean galvanized pail and add one capsule to each square foot of soil. If the soil is dry, I moisten each layer, alternating soil layers and capsules. When the last layer and capsule have been placed, I cover the container and store where it is protected from freezing. After two weeks, I dump the soil out to aerate for a few days before using.

## LIGHT, A KEY TO GOOD GROWTH

Geraniums need strong light to produce compact growth and abundant blooms. Indoors, especially in winter, they need to be grown in sunny south or east windows. Here in Minnesota, the sun shining on the snow reflects into the windows and gives added brightness. But we have many gloomy overcast days, too, and sometimes it is difficult to get heavy bloom during December and January. Rotate window-grown geraniums twice a week to keep them from leaning toward the sun.

6. *Zonal geraniums bloom profusely along with blue lobelia in planter box of south-facing sun porch.* PHOTO BY PAUL E. GENEREUX

Summer is quite another thing. Geraniums growing indoors in sunny spots often need the protection of light curtains to prevent foliage burn during the summer.

Outdoors, grow geraniums in full sun and give them ample water. When roots are kept moist the top growth can stand as much sunlight as zinnias. There are exceptions, of course, and they are mentioned in chapters dealing with particular types of geraniums and pelargoniums.

The fluorescent-lamp way of lighting geraniums is discussed in Chapter 14.

## MOISTURE REQUIREMENTS

Geraniums require less water than many other plants (African violets, begonias, and azaleas, for example). Too much or too little water causes leaves to turn yellow and drop. Water geraniums thoroughly from the top, then do not water again until the surface of the soil feels dry to the touch. If you cannot judge the soil by feeling it (this seems difficult for novice gardeners), purchase a moisture meter to tell you when the plants need water. Use the meter according to directions. Test the soil on outdoor plants the day after watering; on indoor plants two or three days after watering. A reading of "slightly moist" indicates the best soil condition.

In northern areas, winter-grown plants which are subjected to low-light intensity need to become nearly dry between waterings. As the sun grows stronger in the new year, the plants can stand heavier watering.

If you grow dozens of potted geraniums, consider the use of a *soil detergent* to cut down the watering chore. When applied to the soil according to manufacturer's directions, this product keeps soil moist for longer periods of time and makes dry soil absorb water faster. I have used this material on the soil of geraniums in all stages of growth—seedlings, cuttings, newly-potted, and mature plants—and have found it to be a real time-saver and nontoxic to the plants. However, as with any new product or method, try it on a few plants before using it on your entire collection.

Geraniums will grow under conditions of low relative humidity, but they flower best when the relative humidity is maintained at 40 to 50 percent. If grown in dry air the leaves often turn brown and

7. *This view from a shaded part of the designer Edith Head's terrace shows golden marguerites with soy tubs of geraniums. The geraniums include fancy-leaved zonals and scenteds, in full sun; note that while the plants are large, they are at the same time compact and flower-covered.* PHOTO FROM WOODWARD RADCLIFFE BY CLYDE McCLARY

flower buds wither before opening. Increase the relative humidity by setting potted plants on saucers of moist sand or trays of moist pebbles, or by placing the pots in larger pots lined with moist sphagnum moss. Some growers keep potted geraniums on bricks which stand in a small amount of water. Indoor fountains through which water circulates continuously are attractive and raise the moisture content of the surrounding air.

When humidity is a problem, it is wise to purchase a humidity indicator, or hygrometer, at the hardware store so that you can determine the amount of moisture in the air around your plants. If the relative humidity is very low, consider an electrically-operated humidifier to add moisture to the air; you and your plants will benefit.

## TEMPERATURE AND VENTILATION

Geraniums thrive in daytime temperatures of 70 to 75 degrees. Night temperatures should be dropped to a range of 60 to 65 degrees if possible. If you must grow your geraniums where temperatures are up in the 80s or down in the 30s, do not try to force them into flower. Keep them slightly dry and dormant until you can move them to a better growing area. Plants near windows, especially in winter, are always cooler than those growing near solid walls. You may find it more comfortable to let the house cool during the night and return to average living-room temperatures during the day. Meanwhile, the plants will thrive.

In warmer areas such as California and Florida, geraniums remain outdoors the year around, for they are perennials. If you live where temperatures dip near freezing, as in parts of Oregon, geraniums wintering outdoors will need to be protected with mulch on the ground, and in cold spells with paper or boxes over the plants. In the Midwest we winter all cultivated geraniums indoors.

If you live in a climate with torrid summers you will find that your indoor geraniums enjoy the air conditioning as much as you do.

In our busy household I do not need to provide special ventilation for window-grown geraniums, because doors are opened frequently each day, admitting fresh air. If you feel that your indoor plants need fresh air in winter, give it to them via a door or window located at some distance from the plants. A blast of frost-laden air will shrivel the tender winter growth.

## FERTILIZING

It is impossible to stipulate rules for fertilizing geraniums. Plants often indicate that they need fertilizer by sending out new yellowish green leaves. When geraniums are in active growth, usually during early spring and all summer, fertilize them once a month with a balanced fertilizer.

Overfertilizing geraniums tends to make them produce an abundance of foliage and few flowers.

Water-soluble houseplant fertilizer is easy to handle when the manufacturer's directions are followed precisely. Apply liquid fertilizer to nicely moist soil—not when the growing medium is already wet, and not when it is bone-dry. If you prefer to use a dry fertilizer, scratch it into the soil, then water the plant.

Many geranium collectors water their plants once a week with a one-fourth strength solution of all-purpose fertilizer. Gardeners who pot plants in sphagnum moss rather than soil usually moisten plants only with a one-tenth strength fertilizer solution instead of with plain water.

Other gardeners use only organic fertilizers such as the fish emulsions, or alternate between them and chemical fertilizers. Manure tea, another organic type, is made by steeping a bag of dehydrated manure in a pail of water; the solution is diluted to the color of weak tea, then applied to plants.

When you have lived with your geraniums for a while, you will recognize their needs and know when they require additional nitrogen for healthy leaf color; more phosphorus to boost flower production; or perhaps trace elements to add to overall perfection.

## CONTAINERS FOR GERANIUMS

Container-grown plants have many advantages. Even gardeners in the deep South and far West who can garden outdoors year-round take advantage of container gardening because of its flexibility in bringing color to all parts of the home landscape. Container gardeners become quick-change artists, replacing nonflowering plants with others in full bloom or changing the color scheme to fit the season. There is a wide choice of containers, all suitable to some degree for geraniums: plain and fancy pots, boxes, tubs, urns, strawberry jars, and hanging baskets.

Ordinary clay pots with ample drainage holes are among the best containers for geraniums, but for added beauty and special displays, consider some of the other types of containers.

Colorful glazed pots with drainage holes enhance the beauty of

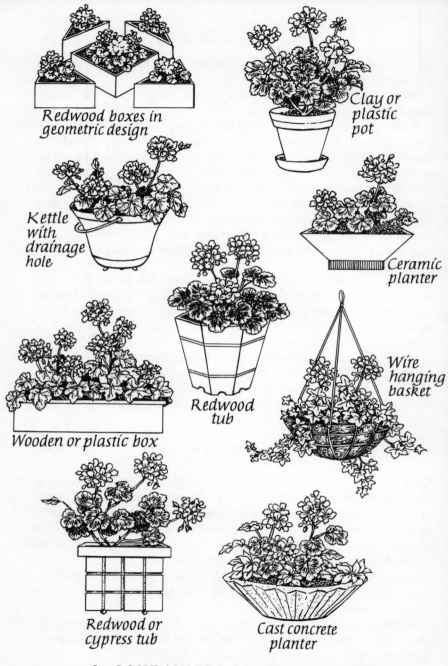

Redwood boxes in geometric design

Clay or plastic pot

Kettle with drainage hole

Ceramic planter

Wooden or plastic box

Redwood tub

Wire hanging basket

Redwood or cypress tub

Cast concrete planter

8. CONTAINERS FOR GERANIUMS

geranium foliage and flowers. Plastic pots are favorites, especially with gardeners who have extensive geranium collections. Plastic pots reduce the watering chore (moisture retention is greater than clay) and they are lightweight. Adversely, a new grower may give plants in plastic pots more water than they need.

Redwood boxes are splendid for geraniums. Boxes and flowers combine to adorn terraces and patios, entryways and foundations. Where indoor space is no problem the boxes can do double duty, gracing windows during winter. Or, consider my plan: at my kitchen door I have a pair of redwood planters that have withstood the rigors of twenty Minnesota winters. They are filled with geraniums in summer, with evergreen branches in winter.

Strawberry jars are marvelous for displaying a collection of miniature or dwarf geraniums. Add an inch or two of broken clay pot chips to the bottom of the jar. Fill the center of the container with a moss stick, a small tube of chicken wire filled with sphagnum moss, or a similar device to simplify top watering. Add soil and plant the geraniums.

Hanging baskets of wood or wire are desirable for displaying ivy-leaved geraniums. The baskets need to be prelined with sheet moss, coarse sphagnum moss, or plastic, then filled with the soil mixture.

The gardener on a budget will be happy to hear that some of the healthiest geraniums I have ever seen were grown in tin cans. To develop this idea, punch several drainage holes in the bottom of each can, then apply colored enamel to the outside.

# 3

# Potting, Pruning, and Propagating Geraniums

Watching my plants thrive, shifting them from small pots to larger quarters, propagating plants so I can have quantities of my favorites, and pruning and snipping plants to pleasing contours—these are my greatest gardening joys. Geraniums oblige me in all these ways, for they grow rapidly with good care, they are easily propagated, and they respond readily to seasonal pruning.

## POTTING AND TRANSPLANTING

Geraniums flower best when they are slightly potbound. Science explains it this way: whatever tends to check the extension of other [geranium] parts favors the development of flowers. Frequent transplanting tends to produce dwarf geraniums.

Geraniums purchased in three-inch pots will be ready for an immediate shift to five-inch pots. Start with clean pots. I like to wash old pots in a solution of a combination insecticide and fungicide which disinfects and cleans away algae. Pots also come clean when scrubbed with hot soapy water.

Soak new clay pots in water overnight before using, otherwise they will pull the moisture out of the soil and away from the roots.

If your soil mix contains a large proportion of sand, insert sphagnum moss in the drainage hole to keep soil from washing out. Cover the drainage hole in the bottom of the pot with a piece of broken clay pot, rounded side up. Add a half inch of clay pot chips to a five-inch pot, and you are ready to pot new plants or transplant old ones.

9. *Repot rootbound geranium in pot one size larger. If new pot is over four inches in diameter, use piece of crock or rough stone over drainage hole.* PHOTO BY MERRY GARDENS

10. *Center plant and fill pot with moist soil.* PHOTO BY MERRY GARDENS

11. *Press soil firmly about the roots, but do not pack tightly.* PHOTO BY MERRY GARDENS

To transplant, hold the lower part of the plant with one hand, and with the other hand give the pot base a sharp whack against a table or board to dislodge the plant and rootball. If plants are very rootbound, break the pot to free the rootball. To prevent the stunting that results from spiraling root growth, make three one-quarter-inch vertical slashes on the sides of the rootball. Hold the plant over the new pot with one hand, add soil to the bottom of the pot with the other hand. Lower the plant into the fresh soil and continue to add soil until the plant is centered and approximately one inch of space is left between the top surface of the soil and the pot rim. Do not pack a heavy soil tightly, as subsequent waterings will do the job for you. Do pack a peat moss mixture fairly tightly; water will still run through it freely.

## PINCHING AND PRUNING

When your geraniums grow too tall and rangy, simply cut off top growth to the desired height. Within a week or so new leaves will appear below the cut area. Stop cutting back or pinching at least three months before you want bloom from your plants. For mid-spring blooms, pinch out tips until February; for fall and winter blooms, pinch or cut back plants in August and September.

If you have tall, leggy plants, cut them down to two or three nodes or joints with a sharp knife. New growth will spring from the remaining plant. If you hesitate to trim them so drastically, cut back to the last pair of leaves, then as new growth emerges in lower areas continue to cut the plant back to the desired height.

The regal *Pelargoniums,* or Lady Washington geraniums, are an exception to these rules: to avoid loss of spring bloom, prune them only in early fall.

The cuttings you remove will furnish material for summer-bedding or winter-window gardens. Starting plants from cuttings is not difficult and will be discussed later.

Geraniums growing in the open garden (or in large pots) often develop tremendous root systems. When you lack space to accommodate such large plants or pots, yet want to keep all or part of them, trim the tops as suggested above, then prune the roots to fit smaller pots. It there are several old trunks growing in one pot, separate them by pulling, or chop them apart with a sharp knife. Repot in fresh soil and give them plenty of light. Within two months they will be strong, bushy plants.

## Grooming Aged Geraniums

Who can deny the beauty of a four- or five-foot geranium, clothed in healthy green leaves and glowing with bright blossom clusters? With a minimum application of tender loving care it is possible to help all geraniums age gracefully. At Como Park Conservatory, St. Paul, Minnesota, Supervisor Robert Schweitze maintains dozens of old geraniums in beautiful condition by growing them cool and somewhat dry during winter, then bringing them into flower for early spring. These tall plants grow in eight- and ten-inch pots. Some have as many as five main stems, all tied to a central stake.

12. *Author's four-foot pillar type zonal geranium. Although the plant is eight years old, note vigorous leaf growth and profuse quantity of flowers.* PHOTO BY MEL JACOBSEN

The care of these aged geraniums approximates that recommended for *Pelargonium hortorum,* the garden geranium. Tops are neatly cut back in the fall so they will be ready for spring bloom, and the plants are fertilized once a month during their growing season with one of the balanced houseplant fertilizers.

I have some large geraniums which I prize for patio color in spring and summer, and for garden fillers while waiting for tall chrysanthemums to flower. 'Minnetonka,' an older variety with semidouble rosy-salmon flowers which often sport to pale salmon and white, stands four feet above the pot line after its fall pruning session. During summer it raises flower heads a foot higher than this.

Double-flowering white 'Mme. Buchner,' a five-year-old, is the same size and has three main stems or trunks, the largest of which is nearly an inch across.

In the novelty class there is fast-growing 'Mr. Wren,' with rounded, light-red florets edged in white. It was grown from seed and now, at the grand old age of four years, stands well over three feet tall and is nicely branched, its silvery trunk an inch in diameter.

New growth constantly springs around the base of an old plant. I encourage one or two of the strongest of these basal shoots to grow, to cover what might otherwise be bare trunk areas.

If you would like to try grooming one of the older plants, I will wager that you can obtain one in the fall when gardeners are putting their gardens to bed. It is then that the big plants hit the compost pile, when gardeners remove a cutting or two for spring bloom and discard the old plant.

# PROPAGATING GERANIUMS

It is always fun to get something for nothing and that is what happens when we grow new plants from cuttings taken from our favorite geraniums. Geraniums can be propagated through stem and leaf cuttings, plant division, air layering, grafting, and seed. The vegetative methods such as cuttings, division, and layering assure that the new plant will be a replica of its parent. With grafting, it is possible to "weld" one or more varieties to a common stock. Seedlings, except those of species, do not come true to parental form. While they are much fun to grow, their exact color and contour cannot be predicted.

## Cuttings

Four- to six-inch tip or side cuttings are easy to handle and will root quickly, but you can root cuttings as small as one-half inch or as tall as eighteen inches. Use a sharp clean knife to take cuttings. Cut directly below a node, strip the lower leaves from the cutting, and insert the cutting in a moistened, pasteurized medium. Geranium cuttings root easily in coarse sand, vermiculite, sponge rock, sphagnum moss, in a combination of all of these plus one-half-part peat moss, or in just plain water. Some geranium growers root cuttings in other media, such as coal ashes, sawdust, bagasse (residue from burnt sugarcane) or plain soil.

It is not necessary to dip cuttings in hormone powder. Geraniums are powerful growers. Failure to root is sometimes due to the use of strong hormone rooting aids. If you want to use a hormone powder, mix it half-and-half with talcum powder, then dip cuttings and plant them immediately.

Pot several cuttings in a bulb pan or squatty azalea pot, or pot singly in two-inch clay or peat pots.

Give the cuttings light shade during the two or three weeks it takes to form roots. To window gardeners, this means keeping the cuttings in a well-lighted area out of the direct sun. Fluorescent light gardeners can place cuttings directly under the tubes.

If you set cuttings outdoors, spray them with a liquid that has been formulated to retard water loss in plants.

When rooted, the cuttings can be set in full sunlight. I like to place individual pots of cuttings in a large pan of sand. I keep the sand well moistened and it transfers the water to the cuttings. Otherwise, cuttings need to be watered only enough to keep them firm and to prevent shriveling.

Always on the lookout for space-saving methods for indoor gardening, I discovered I could root geranium cuttings with the plastic roll method or in individual plastic bags, just as I root many African violets, begonias, and other plants. You can use any untreated plastic film, even the kind used by dry cleaners to protect clothing. A piece of plastic film six inches wide by eighteen inches long will handle six to eight cuttings. Lay the plastic flat and place a half-inch-thick layer of moist sphagnum moss in a strip down the center of the plastic. Space the geranium cuttings on the moss and cover the ends with another half-inch layer of moist moss. Fold the bottom edge of the plastic over the stems of the cuttings and fasten

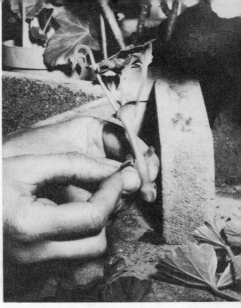

13. *Use clean, sharp knife to take tip cuttings of healthy growth; cut directly below a node.* PHOTO BY MERRY GARDENS

14. *Remove lower leaves and stipules (as shown) from base of cutting.* PHOTO BY MERRY GARDENS

15. *If you wish to use a root-inducing hormone, mix it half-and-half with talcum powder, then dip cuttings in this just before planting.* PHOTO BY MERRY GARDENS

16. *Insert cutting in moistened, pasteurized medium (sand is shown).* PHOTO BY MERRY GARDENS

the ends with staples or tape. Now start rolling the plastic as you would a jelly roll. When you have a neat little bundle, insert it in a small pot or anyplace where the cuttings can stand upright. These rolls need no additional watering until cuttings are ready to transplant. Small plastic bags make marvelous individual pots for cuttings. Place any favorite rooting medium in the bag with the cutting and close with a rubber band around the stem.

As cuttings in pots, pans, or plastic become potbound, shift them to three- or four-inch pots of soil.

Leaf cuttings take a month or two longer to develop into flowering plants, but this is a good way to propagate rare plant material. Make the cutting so a leaf is left on one joint. To be on the safe side, select leaves that show some swelling at the node. These are mallet cuttings, with the stem acting as the mallet head and the leaf as the handle. Leaf cuttings are rooted as suggested for other cuttings.

## Air Layering

An old rangy geranium can be turned into a shorter specimen by air layering. With a sharp knife, cut a slash directly below a node on the main stem. Place wet sphagnum moss around the stem, covering the slash. Wrap plastic film around the moss and tie it to the stem with plastic ties at top and bottom. Roots will form at the slashed section and grow into the moss. When strong root growth appears—from two to six weeks depending on the age of the plant—cut off the rooted portion and plant it in a pot of soil.

## Grafting

If you have ever done grafting on fruit trees, roses, or other ornamental plants, you can use the same procedure to graft geraniums. If you have never done any plant grafting, why not try it? It is inexpensive, easy once you learn how, and you can accomplish wonders with grafted geraniums. With grafting it is possible to produce several different colored blooms on one plant; to grow in weeks tree forms which ordinarily take months; and to produce tall standards topped with lovely trailing ivy-leaved types. I have pink, white, and salmon single and double flowers blooming from grafts on a single geranium plant! This is indeed a novelty item, and it causes much comment among friends who have never tried grafting plants.

Michael D. Paulsen, a horticultural student at the University of

Wisconsin, Madison, has written a paper on "Geranium Grafting." An issue of *Geraniums Around the World,* publication of the International Geranium Society, mentioned grafted novelties which were the hit of the show at Santa Barbara, California . . . "A large pot of fancy-leaved 'Lady Pollock' grafted to a strong *P. domesticum;* 'Fiat Enchantress' grafted to 'Mme. Buchner' with both scion and stock blooming simultaneously, making an enchanting arrangement in pink and white."

The plant to which material is being grafted is called the stock. The material being grafted to it is the scion.

Half-ripened wood from a two-year-old plant makes fine scionwood. The grafting can be done at any time of the year but the scion and the stock must be in the same stage of growth. Prepare the stock by cutting off all leafy growth at any point where the wood is semiripe. To make the incision for the scion, use a sharp knife and make a vertical cut an inch long in the center of the stem. Prepare the scion from a cutting containing three or four nodes. Make slanting cuts at the base of the scion, so it is wedge-shaped. It is best to have scion the same diameter as the stock, but grafting can be done when the scion is smaller if the cambium layers (the thin green layer between bark and wood) are brought into direct contact with the cambium of the stock.

Grafting is fine, too, for rejuvenating old geraniums. New growth (scions) can be whip-grafted near joints. Make a slanting cut on the stock and the same type of cut on the scion and place the pair together. They must fit evenly. The graft can be tied with raffia or plastic strips or held in place with grafting wax or with non-medicated adhesive tape.

After grafting, cover the grafts with a small plastic bag secured with wire or tied with plastic strips. Set the plants in a humid atmosphere for a few days to keep the scion from wilting.

It usually takes two to three weeks for the grafted parts to grow together. Then remove the material covering the wound and the grafted areas should appear as one, or very nearly so.

## GROWTH STIMULANTS AND REGULATORS

Gibberellic acid, now available to home gardeners in aerosol cans, will increase geranium foliage growth, hasten floral formation, and lengthen the life of flowers. It will also increase the size of the

17. *Three steps in doing a geranium side graft.* PHOTO BY DEPARTMENT OF HORTICULTURE, *University of Wisconsin.*

flower trusses if used at the correct time on plants which are, and have been, growing under optimum conditions.

Spray the florets of umbels (flat or round flower clusters) when the first few begin to open and show color. Spray according to the manufacturer's directions and you will note an increase in petal size and pedicel length and will enjoy longer-lasting flowers.

R. H. Lindstrom and S. H. Wittwer, Michigan State University, East Lansing, did considerable work with gibberellic acid and geraniums. An excellent account of this work has been published in *Geraniums Around the World.*

A hobbyist from Schuyler, Nebraska, reports that she ruined a complete collection of variegated-leaved geraniums by spraying them too heavily and too often with gibberellic acid.

Professor Lindstrom has also done some work with Cycocel in geraniums. He mentions that the chemical reduces the height of the geraniums.

If you want to try any of these new chemicals go slowly, follow manufacturer's instructions to the letter, and start with plants you can afford to lose, for there is always a chance that the experiments may not be successful.

# 4

## *Hybridizing Geraniums*

How exciting it is to read about a new plant or to discover one in a nursery or greenhouse. It is a hundred times more exciting to discover a new variety growing in your own garden!

New varieties sometimes occur when a plant mutates or "sports." A portion of the plant (foliage, flowers, or both) is different from the rest of the plant. Nature creates many new geranium varieties in this manner. Outstanding among mutations are the many sports of double red geranium 'Ricard,' which some firms list as 'Improved Ricard.'

'Red Cloud,' to be introduced soon by Fred Bode, Jr., is a sport of 'Pink Cloud,' which was developed at Iowa State University and is the twelfth most popular geranium on the market. The Royal Fiat group, outstanding for their sharply serrated petals, sport back and forth from carnation-like flowers to plain rounded petal edges.

Mutations may result from chemical or physical changes in genes, or from a change in the number or structure of chromosomes. This occurs frequently in nature and can be induced artificially by the use of the chemical colchicine, or by subjecting plants or seeds to X-ray treatments. The mutants can be increased in quantity by cutting off and rooting the sporting branch. Usually the new plant will retain its different foliage, flower, and growth habits, as will future propagations made from it.

## HOW TO HYBRIDIZE GERANIUMS

New geranium cultivars are most frequently produced by hybridization between two selected geranium plants.

Before attempting any plant breeding, it is good to know something about the parts of the flowers.

The five or more green points surrounding the base of a geranium flower are called *sepals*. They form the *calyx* which protects the small flower bud. In nature, *florets,* which consist of five to fifteen or more colored petals, and the *nectary* at the base of the blossom, attract birds and insects which carry pollen from one flower to another, thus causing flowers to set seed. If we want seed from our geraniums, we must duplicate this pollinating process by transferring pollen from the anthers of one floret to the stigma of another floret.

Commercial growers who require large quantities of seed to sell often make large plantings of like types of geraniums in one general area. When the birds and insects work among the flowers, they pollinate on a large scale and the grower can harvest a fine crop of naturally pollinated seed.

The amateur hybridizer or plant breeder will want to select for parents those plants with superior qualities such as vigorous growth, unusually fine foliage, floriferousness, or striking floral coloring or pattern.

Centered in each floret are the female elements: an elongated object called the *pistil,* with the *ovaries* at its base. The tip of the pistil expands to five small arching parts known as the *stigma*. This central column is surrounded by the male element, a ring of *stamens,* some of which are tipped with pollen-bearing sacs.

All that is necessary to make most geraniums produce seed is to transfer pollen from one floret to another with a small brush, the tip of the finger, or a pair of tweezers. To prevent self-pollination of your geraniums, snip off the anthers of the floret selected to be the seed parent before they expand and ripen. When the pollen has been transferred, cover the pollinated floret with a small transparent bag and mark it with a tag showing name of pollen parent and date of pollination. This reference will be useful if any of the seedlings resulting from the cross are fine enough to name or register.

If you want to hybridize two geraniums which flower at different times, remove the pollen anthers from the earliest-flowering plant and store them in the open for five days to a week. If needed for a longer period, place the pollen inside capsules, label and insert in a jar of silica gel (a chemical dessicant you can buy at the

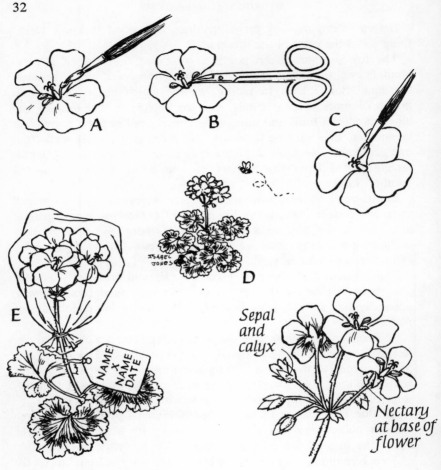

Sepal
and
calyx

Nectary
at base of
flower

## 18. HOW TO HYBRIDIZE GERANIUMS

(A) Use brush to transfer powdery pollen from the male parent to the tip of the pistil of the female or seed-bearing parent (C). To guard against self-pollination, cut off the anthers of the floret selected as seed parent before they expand and ripen (B). (D) Bees often pollinate geraniums growing in the open. The resulting seeds may produce interesting results if you harvest them just before they are completely dry. (E) After pollination it is a wise precaution to cover the pollinated flower with a small transparent bag and mark it with a tag showing name of seed parent and pollen parent and date.

drugstore) and store in the refrigerator. I have kept geranium pollen viable for two weeks in this manner.

It takes four to six weeks for seed capsules or pods to ripen. They vary in size from the five-eighths inch *Pelargonium odoratissimum* pod to the one-and-one-half-inch hybrid seedcase.

When the seedpod is ripe, cut it off and store it in a cool dry place. Seed usually remains viable for ten to twelve months and sometimes longer.

## NAMING NEW CULTIVARS

If you obtain a beautiful cultivar (variety) which you believe is different enough from existing plants to be named, obtain information on naming and registration from the International Geranium Society, 1413 Bluff Drive, Santa Barbara, California.

Many hybrid forms have been produced and named, but there is always a demand for new and different cultivars, as well as for more floriferous and disease-resistant plants.

In a nineteenth-century issue of *Floricultural Cabinet and Florist Magazine,* I discovered some notes which mention a "race of yellows," and a "magnificent Cape species with large panicles of golden yellow flowers." Recently I saw two rare yellow-flowered pelargonium species: tuberous-rooted *P. rapaceum* with ferny leaves and clusters of yellow flowers resembling sweet peas, and *P. ranunculophyllum,* a South African import with hairy, deeply-zoned leaves and pale yellow flowers. Perhaps hybrid forms between these species and other geraniums can be bred to make fine novelty plants.

Fred A. Bode, Jr., owner of Bode's Southern California Geranium Gardens, engages in wholesale plant breeding and shipping. He reports that we can expect great things from the almost everblooming 'Irenes,' a race of floriferous garden and pot geraniums. The new plants will have full, round, double flowers. 'Toyon' is a new 'Irene' that bears enormous umbels of clear scarlet and was named for a holly native to California.

Light rose-red 'Shocking' is another new 'Irene,' and while this color is not so popular with geranium fanciers, I have seen 'Shocking' in numerous collections. Mr. Bode expects to bring out several more interesting and floriferous 'Irene' types.

## FROM SEED TO FLOWER

Seed of the various types of pelargoniums may be purchased from specialists. Starting plants from seed is the easy, inexpensive way to increase your collection.

As I write this I can look at a "plantation" of 'Little Read's' seedlings, which may become very dwarf, bushy plants. This is how fast they grow: ten seeds were planted on October 5; two seeds germinated on October 15 and the others in rapid succession. Two weeks from planting time, nine sturdy plants were showing and a small hump in the soil indicated that the tenth one would push into the world on the fifteenth day. We do not always get one hundred percent germination, but seed is reasonably priced and we usually get more seedlings than we can handle.

Hasten germination of geranium seed by removing the brown husk encasing the seed, or prick the husk with a pin so water can penetrate. Otherwise, it may take weeks or even months for the seed to germinate. Advanced growers often clip the ends of seeds to speed germination.

19. *Prepare flat for sowing seeds by adding layer of broken crock, pebbles, or coarse sphagnum moss for drainage, then screen soil mixture to within one inch of the top.* PHOTO BY BURPEE SEEDS

20. *Add half-inch layer of horticultu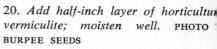 vermiculite; moisten well.* PHOTO BURPEE SEEDS

21. *Mark rows in vermiculite, one-quarter inch deep and about two inches apart.* PHOTO BY BURPEE SEEDS

22. *Hasten germination of geranium seed by removing the brown husk that encases the seed, or prick the husk with a pin so water can penetrate more readily.* PHOTO BY BURPEE SEEDS

23. *When seedlings have set of true leaves, transplant into small pots of moist geranium soil.* PHOTO BY BURPEE SEEDS

Plant seed in vermiculite, sand, sphagnum moss, perlite, or sterilized porous soil. Press the seed into the medium and cover with about a quarter-inch layer of mixture. Germination may be sporadic, with some seedlings appearing in as few as four days and others taking up to six months or even longer to show leaves. Cover the planting with a piece of glass or a transparent plastic bag and put in a light, but not bright, place to germinate. When seedlings begin dotting the soil, place the planting on a sunny windowsill or about four inches below fluorescent light tubes.

Transplant seedlings as soon as they are large enough to handle. They grow rapidly and many will be ready for transplanting into two-inch pots of soil when they are two weeks old. They will need another shift to three- or four-inch pots before flowering time.

Continue to keep the planting medium moist and chances are good that you will be rewarded with a few new green sprouts weekly or monthly.

Give growing seedlings ample light, as from an east or south window, water them when the surface of the soil feels dry, fertilize them every second week with quarter-strength water-soluble houseplant fertilizer.

Geraniums often bloom five months after seed sowing, but the average windowsill gardener will find that it takes six to eight months from seed to flower.

24. *First blooms from geranium seedlings come in from five to eight months. This shows a typical flower from Floradale Fancy Mixed zonal geranium seeds.* PHOTO BY BURPEE SEEDS

# 5

# *Geranium Diseases and Pests*

Geraniums growing outdoors and in crowded greenhouses are exposed to numerous diseases and pests, but this is not cause for alarm. Follow basic good-health precautions and practices and your geraniums will fall prey to very few of their enemies.

Purchase your plants from reputable dealers. Isolate all new plants for at least two weeks before placing them among your other plants. Keep a few remedies on hand to check simple diseases and destroy pests if they appear.

Remove spent flowers and faded leaves. If a pest or disease attacks one of your geraniums, isolate the plant and scrub your hands before handling healthy plants.

Simple pesticides and precautionary dusts are good to have on hand in the event of trouble. I use the aerosol houseplant bombs to eradicate most pests, but I also keep malathion, DDD, and fermate or a similar compound to dust or drench on propagating media or on soil in which rhizoctonia (crown or root rot) might exist.

## DISEASES

The University of California has published a definitive bulletin, "Diseases of Geraniums in California," by Albert O. Paulus, Donald E. Munnecke, and the late Philip A. Chandler. Some of the diseases described are likely to occur wherever geraniums are grown and I have drawn freely from this bulletin.

Dr. Frank P. McWhorter, plant pathologist with the Oregon Agricultural Experiment Station, Corvallis, and the Agricultural Research Service, United States Department of Agriculture, has written several papers related to verticillium in geraniums. One especially fine paper, "Verticillium Control Must Be Considered When Indexing Geraniums," appeared in the May 10, 1962, issue of *Florists'*

*Review.* With permission, I have quoted directly from this story. **Verticillium.** Quoting Fred Bode, Jr., "Some rather radical changes have been made in the understanding about [pelargonium] diseases, especially in regard to bacterial stem-rot which was until recently not divided from verticillium. [Verticillium organisms of this soil-borne disease grow in the water-conducting tissue, poisoning the plant and causing it to wilt.] Now it is understood that bacterial stem-rot is of very little importance when good culture is practiced but verticillium, a disease of the soil and very common in gardens, makes the best gardener vulnerable to great loss."

As it is almost impossible for the average gardener to distinguish between these two diseases (verticillium and stem rot), every effort should be made to keep plants in healthy growing condition, keeping soil sterilized and discarding all plants showing symptoms of disease. Do not take cuttings from infected stock. The cuttings may live for a short time but they are carriers of the disease and may spread it among your other geraniums.

Verticillium is a soil fungus which enters geraniums through their

## 25. VERTICILLIUM SYMPTOMS

*(A) Stems necrosed by verticillium are unlikely to produce terminal leaves. (B) Leaf of verticillium-infected geranium may show yellowing like this along veins to edge. (C) Yellowed leaves cup unnaturally and will soon fall as the verticillium progresses.*

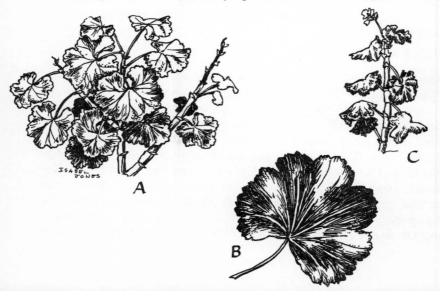

roots. It is often confused with bacterial rots, and indeed many of the symptoms are similar. Verticillium-infected plants show dwarfing, leaf-yellowing which is brighter yellow than that of botrytis-infected plants, and wilt. *P. domesticum* and scented-leaved cultivars rarely become wilted but they do develop yellow-spotted foliage. Older leaves on ivy-leaved geraniums lose color, turn gray-brown and still cling to the plant.

According to Dr. Frank P. McWhorter, "Planting of stock plants in outdoor locations where the soil is infested with verticillium is the most likely method of infection. This is especially true in florists' cultures if the bedding area chosen has grown composites, especially dahlias." There is no known cure for verticillium-infected plants. Dr. McWhorter suggests these controls: "Select apparently virus-free plants; culture index cuttings from these plants for bacteria verticillium; grow stock plants for at least two generations in sterilized soil."

**Bacterial Leaf Spot and Stem Rot.** Bacterial leaf spot and stem rot are caused by *Xanthomonas pelargoni.* This bacterium attacks leaves and stems of plants, and cuttings of *P. hortorum* and *P. peltatum,* but it does not affect *P. domesticum.*

Leaf infection shows in round spots or large, angular dead areas.

Small water-soaked spots on the undersides of leaves symptomize round leaf spot. Within two or three days spots become slightly indented and the leaf wilts and dies. The disease may spread to leaves and into the stem or it may check itself, as some varieties are immune to the disease.

This disease may manifest itself by killing an angular section of the leaf. Leaf edges wilt and in a week or two the leaf dies and falls from the plant. Angular leaf killing is only one step away from stem rot.

**Stem Rot or Black Rot.** This is the scourge of geranium growers. Infected stems blacken and shrivel. If cut open these areas show a crumbly black rot. Black streaks along the stems show the presence of the bacteria in the vascular or water-carrying system. As the disease progresses, plants suffer heavy loss of foliage until, in advanced stages, the only foliage remaining will be small leaves at branch tips.

Bacteria-infected cuttings slowly rot from the base upward and in two to four weeks after cuttings have been struck, stems show the dull black-brown or stem rot.

The disease is spread by knives which have been contaminated

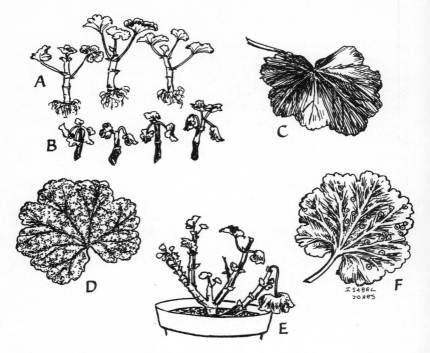

## 26. GERANIUM DISEASES

*(A) healthy cuttings (B) diseased cuttings (C) angular leaf spot (D) measles, a virus disease (E) black stem rot or blackleg (F) round leaf spot*

in taking cuttings from infected plants, by handling plants, and by splashing water on plants.

There is no known cure for this disease. Destroy infected plants and sterilize all tools which may have been used on infected plants by dipping them for a minute in 1:1000 mercuric chloride (corrosive sublimate) solution. This highly poisonous chemical is obtainable in tablet form at drugstores. Handle it with care and keep it away from children and pets.

**Other Leaf Spots.** In addition to the bacterial leaf spot already described, botrytis leaf- and blossom-blight and gray mold also affect geraniums. Flower petals turn brown prematurely and drop onto the leaves. The leaf area under the dead blossoms becomes brown and moldy. A pocket microscope or magnifying glass will reveal the gray-brown mold.

Botrytis-infected leaves do not wilt and hang from the stem

limply, as in bacterial leaf spot. Botrytis usually affects older leaves first, and generally confines itself to a few leaves rather than spreading through the entire plant.

Control botrytis leaf spot by removing all dead leaves and flowers. The disease is more prevalent among plants growing in cold, wet, poorly ventilated areas. Raise the temperature, lower the humidity, provide better ventilation, and space plants so they do not crowd one another.

Spray with captan, eight teaspoonfuls per gallon of water, at five- to seven-day intervals.

**Virus Diseases.** Virus diseases in geraniums are as complex and as baffling as those affecting people. They appear more often in winter than in summer. There are no known cures, only controls.

Foliage affected with mosaic virus becomes dotted with light and dark green areas. The virus usually spreads through the entire plant and is carried in cuttings.

Leaf curl, also known as crinkle or measles, is characterized by pale yellow spots, foliage crinkling and dwarfing, with leaves finally yellowing and dropping.

Marginal leaf roll or leaf cupping are symptoms of curly top, a virus transmitted by the beet leafhopper.

Control virus diseases by propagating with disease-free cuttings from a mother block. (See Chapter 3.) Geranium seed appears to be virus-free.

**Cutting Rot (Blackleg).** Symptoms are brown water-soaked lesions at the base of cuttings. Soon the area enlarges, turns black, and extends upward into the cutting. The affected area is often wet and slimy and the leaves yellow and fall from the cutting.

Control the disease by taking tip cuttings from healthy plants. Dip them for ten minutes in a fungicide, such as a solution of two tablespoons of fermate to a gallon of water. Root them in pasteurized soil. Any device which hastens rooting, such as a heating cable to raise the bottom temperature, will cut down losses due to blackleg.


# PESTS


**Aphids.** Aphids, small black or green plant lice, appear on new growth. Destroy those on window-grown plants with a houseplant aerosol bomb, or dip the tops of plants into soapy water.

**Red Spider.** Many geranium growers will never encounter geranium foliage marred by red spider. However, this pest is common in some areas, especially during winter when temperatures are high and humidity is low, and again during summer when plants may be growing outdoors. This pest, so small a magnifying glass is needed to see it, causes yellow-and-brown areas on foliage. Eradicate red spider by spraying the plants with an aerosol houseplant bomb or with a spray formulated to control spider mites. If the infestation is light, spray upper and under sides of leaves with cold water.

**Mealy Bugs.** Mealy bugs look like specks of cotton. If you find only a few on your plants, kill them by touching each with a small swab dipped in rubbing alcohol, nail-polish remover, or cologne. If the infestation is heavy, spreading into leaf axils, stipules, and flowers, eradicate them with malathion or a heavy spraying from an aerosol bomb.

**Caterpillars.** Tobacco budworms, green or pinkish caterpillars which hatch from eggs laid by moths, damage flowers by boring into buds and dining on the tender petals. Eradicate the eggs and worms by dusting plants weekly with DDD or DDT.

Orange tortrix, small stout-bodied moths, lay eggs on geraniums and other plants which hatch into small brown-headed caterpillars. These feed on buds and tender new foliage. DDD or malathion will kill them.

**White Fly.** Very small white flies often group together on the underside of leaves, sapping their strength and causing leaves to turn yellow and drop from the plant. Spray with a houseplant aerosol bomb or with malathion mixed according to directions. Repeat at five-day intervals until the pests are eliminated.

**Nematodes.** Nematodes or eelworms are not visible to the naked eye, yet they can do fatal damage to plants. They manifest themselves by stunting the growth of plants, sometimes showing in small nodules or blisters on leaves. If you suspect nematodes, knock the plant free from the pot and examine the roots. You will find that nematode-infested plants have small nodules or swellings along the roots.

Discard and burn nematode-infested plants. Do not use the soil again, and scrub the pots with boiling water before re-use. If the plants are rare or irreplaceable, you may be able to get nematode-free tip cuttings. Plant the cuttings in soil that has been treated with a nemacide such as VC-13 or M-712.

# 6

## *Wintering Geraniums*

Geraniums are perennials and where winter temperatures never fall to freezing they can be wintered outdoors just as any hardy perennial. Where temperatures fall below freezing, geranium enthusiasts must find a way to bring their plants through the winter.

Potted geraniums may be wintered on the windowsill or under fluorescent light. Take cuttings in early fall and start new plants for winter window gardens.

Many gardeners enjoy the beauty of large plants—the kind you just can't grow in one season—but lack indoor gardening space. This problem may be solved by storing the geraniums. Remove them from the pots in the fall and hang them head down from basement rafters. Do not cut back before storing. Sprinkle the rootballs with water every other week. I have seen some remarkable results from this method of storage, even in dry basements. My brother, who lives in Virginia, stores many geraniums this way and they always come through beautifully. When he lived in North Dakota he achieved the same fine results. But I have heard of more failures than successes with this method of storage. Anthony C. Ayton, commenting on this method of wintering geraniums in the August 1963 issue of the *Royal Horticultural Society Journal,* writes, "The plants are so long recovering from this treatment that it is a waste of time." If plants are watered, fertilized, and pruned from early spring until late fall, it is possible to winter them this way until they become too large or too gnarled to be pretty.

About a month before plants are to be set out in the spring, they are potted, cut back, watered and fertilized and brought into the light. When danger of frost is over the plants are moved to the garden.

Geranium growers in our Midwestern states winter geraniums by

## 27. IDEAS FOR WINTERING GERANIUMS

(A) Wrap roots in moist sphagnum moss; surround rootball with ventilated plastic bag; tie at top. (B) Hang moss- and plastic-wrapped
plants in well-ventilated place where temperatures will not fall below
40 degrees or rise above about 65 degrees. (C) If moss dries out,
sprinkle so that it is nicely moist, but never drippy wet, throughout
the winter. (D) If space is available, set pots in moist sand on floor of
bright, cool basement; or in sunny window.

removing them from the pots, encasing the rootballs in ventilated plastic bags, securing the bags with plastic ties, and hanging the plants head down from the basement rafters. I even know of gardeners who winter tree geraniums this way. Roots covered with plastic hold moisture well and need merely to be sprinkled with water at monthly intervals.

Another method of storage is to shake the soil from geranium roots, encase the roots in ventilated plastic bags filled with moistened sphagnum moss and peat moss, tie the bags shut, and hang them in any convenient basement, porch, or attic area where temperatures stay above freezing. Sprinkle the roots with water twice a month, or insert a glass wick in the bag and water by letting the medium absorb a little moisture through the wick, or simply by wetting a rather heavy rag and slipping it into the bag.

As an experiment with this latter method, I dug some geraniums in late August and placed the bare roots in plastic bags. Some of the bags were filled with sphagnum moss and peat moss, some with vermiculite and some with sponge rock. Stored in the basement, they received light from average-sized basement windows. Three months after storing, I checked them. Some plants in each of the storage media were blooming. To be sure, the blooms were very small and so were the leaves, but they came through the winter in fine shape.

When any of these upside-down storage methods are used, the plants should be potted a month to six weeks before they are to be moved to the outdoor garden. Soak the roots for forty minutes or so in water to which you have added proper proportions of a soluble fertilizer. Cut tops back to stimulate growth and pot the geraniums in a regular potting mix.

A friend with an unused basement coal bin had it cleaned and covered the floor with a foot-thick layer of coarse sand. He winters his geraniums in the coal bin by plunging the pots in the sand. They are watered lightly a couple of times a month. In April he trims them back and starts moving them to windows. His geraniums always put on a colorful summer show.

Fluorescent lights make it easy to store geraniums in basements, attics, or any other out-of-the-way areas. You can care for your geraniums under lights just as you do those on windowsills, and they will respond with new foliage and flowers.

Many gardeners store garden-grown geraniums in wooden crates, tubs, and baskets of sand. They are set in the basement and

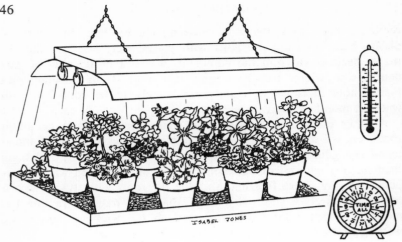

ISABEL JONES

## 28. *WINTERING UNDER FLUORESCENT LIGHT*

*Miniature geraniums are especially adaptable to wintering under fluorescent light. Here a 24-inch reflector with two 20-watt tubes is in use. Thermometer and timer to turn lights on and off automatically are helpful devices.*

watered lightly. If they go into storage in a healthy condition they seem to withstand this rather harsh treatment very well indeed.

If you have good-sized basement windows you might like to winter some of your geraniums in pots at the windows. Treatment is the same as in any window garden except that you will need to grow them somewhat drier and use less fertilizer.

Florida winters usually are warm enough to winter geraniums outdoors, but if a killing frost hits the area, it is possible to salvage some of the plants even though the tops are frozen.

If the weather warms immediately after the freeze, cut back the frozen plant material, mulch the base of the plant with peat moss, straw, leaves, hulls, or ground corncobs. Keep the plant on the dry side until new growth shows, then water and fertilize as usual. Older plants will usually survive a couple of light frosts.

If you live in an area of repeated frosts, dig the plants, cut back all the soft frozen stems, and repot. Water lightly and set them in a well-lighted room. New growth usually shows in about a week or ten days. One year an early August frost blackened my geraniums. I was able to save about fifty percent of the plants in this manner.

# 7

## Heading the Popularity Poll

Gardeners all over the world know the zonal geraniums (*Pelargonium hortorum*), although they may know them as horseshoe, fish, or bedding geraniums. Zonal geraniums adapt wonderfully to both indoor and outdoor gardening. It is no wonder they are so popular: colors include white, pink, salmon, red, lavender, and violet; there are solid-colored flowers, bicolored blossoms, and blooms marked with fancy feathering; and there are single-flowering, semidouble flowering, and full double-flowering zonal geraniums.

The ancestors of our present zonal geraniums were narrow-petaled red, pink, or white *Pelargonium zonale* and red single-flowered *P. inquinans,* which were introduced into England in 1710 and 1714 from South Africa. Double-flowering geraniums came into fashion around 1860. Today the double forms are preferred by most gardeners for outdoor gardens because they do not shatter and lose their petals so easily as the single-flowering plants.

However, there are charm and beauty in the rounded or nearly-pointed petals, the clear colors, and the separation of petals still found on many of the single-flowering plants.

## DOUBLE-FLOWERING GERANIUMS

In Minnesota we garden indoors for eight to nine months of the year and outdoors for three or four months. Small wonder, then, that we select our geraniums for their beauty indoors as well as for their adaptability to outdoor gardens.

Double flowers last longer, and are more wind-resistant, than single flowers. Here, they are grown outdoors in boxes, pots, urns, beds, and landscaped gardens. We find them in city parks, in "community-beautiful" projects, and in gay window gardens.

In some sections of Minneapolis the white and the pink geraniums, such as 'Snowball' and 'Pink Cloud,' are favorites; in the newly developed sections of the city, red-flowered varieties such as 'Better Times,' and 'Ricard' and it hybrid 'Sparkle,' add glow to gardens.

At a large French Provincial estate I saw tubs of light pink 'Princess Fiat,' backed by urns filled with pink hydrangeas. This wealth of pink color pointed up the beauty of a pair of gray-and-blue lead roosters which flanked the steps leading to the household entrance.

Another home featured large pots of azalea-pink 'Dawn,' a semi-double, atop posts leading into a glorious garden of blue delphinium, white ismene (spider lily), and 'Peace' roses.

In a delightful architectural garden, a small square of closely cropped, vivid green grass was bordered with deep pink 'Royal Fiat' geraniums, a variety with serrated, carnation-like petal edges. Elegant blue-and-white ceramic chairs from Portugal were placed invitingly on the grass. A fine planting of blue-flowered clematis 'Ramona' climbed the gray stone walls of the house.

In another garden, a triangular planting of brick-red 'Improved Ricard' bordered with mounds of white alyssum complemented an indoor garden room which featured a round planting of the same red geraniums, pots of variegated peperomia, and statuary.

Red, gold, green, and blue marbles enhanced a terrazo patio floor in a garden of triangular beds of large-trussed, brick-red 'Charlotte' geraniums which pointed up the color of the red marbles.

A delightful, small city garden of my acquaintance blazes with color most of the year. In early spring the borders gleam with bright tulips. When they fade, the bulbs are dug and stored at a nursery and replanted in the fall. The garden is replanted for summer with geraniums, mostly in shades of pink. There are raised beds of rose-pink semidouble 'Genie,' hanging baskets of deep-pink, ivy-leaved 'Charles Turner,' and a half-dozen trees of 'Magnificent,' an apple-blossom-pink geranium with huge flower heads. A narrow border of fragrant, yellow hemerocallis 'Yellowstone' frames this beautiful, unexpected mid-city garden.

One of my favorite gardens is an area between our house and the patio where container-grown plants are beautifully displayed. When blooms start to fade, the plants can be whisked away to the lath house or to a less conspicuous garden area and replaced with other

[1]. *Zonal, fancy-leaved, and scented geraniums blooming in sunny home greenhouse with sweet alyssum, hybrid petunias, and golden coleus.* PHOTO BY ELVIN MCDONALD

[2]. *Zonal geraniums are unrivaled for window-box beauty in the summer. Here light and dark pinks contrast with the blue of browallia.* PAUL E. GENEREUX PHOTO

[3]. *'Dark Red Irene' geraniums inserted in cone-shaped form of water-saturated Oasis on white compote with boxwood and pine-scented geranium leaves makes a gala holiday tree. Author's design.* PHOTO BY MEL JACOBSEN

[4]. *Zonal geraniums growing in small pots and tubs create a cheerful welcome at this garden gate.* PAUL E. GENEREUX PHOTO

[5]. *Even in partial shade outdoors, zonal geraniums do a remarkable work in bringing bright color.* PAUL E. GENEREUX PHOTO

[6]. *In the open garden, zonal geraniums make a good showing alone, or combined with other flowers, like the blue and white ageratum in this garden scene.* PAUL E. GENEREUX PHOTO

[7]. *Ivy-leaved geranium 'Charles Turner' becomes a cascade of beauty when grown in a hanging basket. Here it is seen on a partially sunny terrace in summer.* PAUL E. GENEREUX PHOTO

29. Pelargonium hortorum
*'Fiat Queen'*
PHOTO BY MERRY GARDENS

30. Pelargonium hortorum
*'Pink Cloud'*
PHOTO BY MERRY GARDENS

31. Pelargonium hortorum
*'Princess Fiat'*
PHOTO BY MERRY GARDENS

flowering plants in containers. The color scheme varies, making the most of the plants in flower.

A favorite combination has been a strip of carmine-red hyacinth 'Jan Bos,' planted later with potted dark red geranium 'Irene.' The soil in front of the strip is covered with white crushed rock. A pair of yucca plants which have survived two Minnesota winters are planted in the center of the rock area. Several groupings of cherry-red-flowered, green-and-white-leaved geranium 'Wilhelm Langguth' were bordered by green, gray, and dark red sempervivums. A pair of white-flowered tree-geraniums 'Snowball' added interest to the south corner of this small garden. The north end of the planting had a striking five-foot piece of weathered wood, sprayed moss green. Two shelves were wedged into the wood. Crimson-penciled ivy-leaved geranium 'Princess Victoria' trailed gracefully from the top shelf and 'Willy,' a double-flowering dark red ivy-leaved geranium, grew on the lower shelf. At the end of October we moved some pale golden potted chrysanthemums into this garden and exchanged the red geraniums for salmon-tinted varieties. I hope to experiment with plantings of scented-leaved and miniature geraniums in this small area, using as always the neat-growing little sempervivums for a border. I like the quiet beauty of their prim growth, the perfection of their fine rosette forms, and the way their colors blend with all geraniums.

In California I saw many elegant plantings in which geraniums played the leading roles. Many different forms are used there—single- and double-flowering, trailing, and standard or tree geraniums. Some of the companion plants Californians use with geraniums are not hardy in other areas of the country, but we can substitute shrubs, vines, and perennials of similar color and form to create our own dazzling garden combinations.

Often it is difficult to obtain the correct names of the geraniums used in landscape plantings, and on the tour of California gardens I occasionally had to content myself with taking descriptive notes on the fine combinations. I will pass these notes on to you and you can select named geraniums from catalogs or at nurseries to complete your planting scheme.

Pale salmon geraniums were used to face down several well-pruned peach-flowered hibiscus. Geraniums were planted with single-flowering pink and white chrysanthemums. One garden featured pink carnations, driftwood, and pink and white geraniums.

32. Pelargonium hortorum
*'Apple Blossom'*
PHOTO BY MERRY GARDENS

33. Pelargonium hortorum
*'Honeymoon'*
PHOTO BY MERRY GARDENS

34. Pelargonium hortorum
*'Natalie Webster'*
PHOTO BY MERRY GARDENS

35. Pelargonium hortorum *'Wicked Lady'*
PHOTO BY MERRY GARDENS

Potted golden calendula and crimson-purple geranium 'Star of Persia,' with its slender, twisted petals, made an exciting planting.

I am very fond of day lilies, and it was interesting to see the way Californians use them in combinations with geraniums. One garden had a planting of brown-eyed hemerocallis and related plants such as kniphofia (the poker plant or torch lily), stiffly handsome phormium and blandfordia, bordered with double-flowering white geranium 'Summer Cloud.' Other plantings showed day lilies intermittently spaced with colorful geraniums.

Everywhere there were plantings of lily-of-the-Nile (*Agapanthus umbellatus*) showing its fine blue umbels beside pink or salmon geraniums. The bulbous *Agapanthus* also makes a splendid pot plant which I plan to try as a geranium companion indoors.

Purple-red geranium 'Magenta Ruby' made a spectacular planting at the base of flower-laden bougainvillaea.

The magnificent free-flowering, fast-growing geranium 'Irene,' hybridized by Clarence F. and Irene Behringer, sometimes sports into interesting varieties. Recently I saw a sport of 'Red Irene' with foliage showing netted gold veins and pink zoning. Buds are striped and flowers are semidouble red.

## SINGLE-FLOWERING GERANIUMS

The single-flowering forms of geraniums do shatter more easily than those with double flowers, but to me there is a perfection of form in the single flowers often absent in the big double flowers. Unless some exceptionally windy weather comes along, the single flowers will last a week or more. They are exquisite for flower arrangements, complement annuals and perennials, and are perfect in container gardens.

One of my favorites is large-flowered, garnet-red 'Velma.' I like it for all types of outdoor work and always keep a few in readiness for winter bloom indoors.

'Paul Crampel,' with its resplendent orange-scarlet flowers and fine compact foliage, is an international favorite used wherever bedding geraniums or specimen plants are needed.

A bed or box of low-growing brilliant orange 'Maxime Kovalevski' geraniums adds luster to lawns or gardens.

The large white trusses of geranium 'Marguerite de Layre' add a cool note to summer gardens, and make superb separation plants to divide or enhance colorful red and yellow annuals or perennials.

Plants with picotee flowers (solid color with a marginal band of another color) are among my favorites, whether they are tuberous begonias, amaryllis, or geraniums. 'Carmel' is a luscious white picotee geranium with a red-to-rose margin. It grows into a sumptuous specimen plant.

In Nebraska I saw a planting of pale-orange geranium 'Advance,' melon-colored hemerocallis 'Multnomah,' and pale-blue violas, grown in a raised bed edged with soft-yellow old brick to make an exciting planting.

In California I particularly liked the single-flowered salmon and orange geraniums when they were placed near the exotic orange-and-blue Bird of Paradise (*Strelitzia Reginae*) with its weirdly pointed beaklike flowers. Used at the base of the lovely blue plumbago, or planted near feathery mimosa trees, they were equally effective.

Gardeners who enjoy two-toned flowers will love the single-flowered Painted Lady varieties. All of these beauties have white centers and are margined with pink, red, or fuchsia. 'Salmon Queen' is a standout in my container garden, and deep fuchsia-pink 'Ann Sothern' is beautiful anywhere you want a splash of this vibrant color. In California I saw big bushes of red poinsettias flowering in late May. Planted near them were several pots of single-flowered crimson-red geranium 'General Leonard Wood.' Other Painted Lady varieties favored from Maine to Mexico are light rose-pink 'Alice de la Vergne,' coral-salmon 'Cheerio,' light-red 'Berkeley Belle,' scarlet 'Lady Dryden,' and cerise-red 'Painted Lady.'

## THE FRENCH TYPES OF GERANIUMS

The French-type or Bruant zonal geraniums are more vigorous than others. Foliage is rougher and leaf margins show more serration. Try these strong plants in pots, boxes, or in the garden. They flower freely even when young and their long-lasting flowers make them ideal for arrangements.

One of my favorites in this group is double-flowering salmon-apricot 'Fanfare,' which displays large clusters of enormous flowers in even the hottest summer weather.

The charming 'Fiat' and 'Fiat Queen' are in this group, and they are favorites wherever geraniums are grown. Plants are floriferous, florets are large (two or more inches across), and petal edges are as serrated as those of carnations.

'Blossomtime,' a semidouble salmon-coral French type, has large, smooth flowers which may be light or dark, the color varying with the temperature.

There is no better bedding plant than bushy-leaved salmon-apricot geranium 'Salmon Supreme.' For either pots or gardens, 'Welcome' with its slightly cupped double salmon-coral umbels and strong, handsome foliage is splendid. 'Prize,' a double-red geranium with a white center, bears large clusters of broad-petaled flowers shooting up from its pale green leaves. In the pastel class there are light orchid-pink 'Debonair' and 'Lavender Ricard.'

## FAVORITE DOUBLE AND SEMIDOUBLE GERANIUMS

Fred A. Bode, Jr., Escondido, California, grows and breeds geraniums for the wholesale trade. His ranch is partly the "most arid land in the world and is smack against the ocean. Under such conditions no local plant diseases, pests or foreign pollen-bearing insects are flying." Every year he ships thousands of geraniums all over the world. You will find many of his originations at your nursery or listed in catalogs. Mr. Bode compiled the following list of the twenty-six leading zonal geraniums. It tallies with the lists of favorites I have received from other growers and hobbyists.

## Favorite Zonal Geraniums in Order of Popularity

### (D) DOUBLE FLOWERS        (SD) SEMIDOUBLE FLOWERS

| | | |
|---|---|---|
| 'Irene' | crimson-red | SD |
| 'Dark Red Irene' | vermilion | SD |
| 'Improved Ricard' | light brick-red | SD |
| 'Springtime' | light salmon | SD |
| 'Olympic Red' | clear red | SD |
| 'Fiat Enchantress' | salmon-pink | SD |
| 'Penny' | neon pink | SD |
| 'Genie' | medium rose-pink | SD |
| 'Salmon Irene' | medium salmon | SD |
| 'Snowball' | white | D |
| 'Better Times' | crimson-red | D |
| 'Pink Cloud' | light salmon-pink | SD |
| 'Fiat' | rich salmon | D |
| 'Mme. Buchner' | white | D |
| 'Orange Ricard' | orange shading to scarlet | SD |
| 'A. M. Mayne' | purple | D |
| 'Picardy' | medium salmon-pink to medium salmon | SD |
| 'Red Landry' | light brick-red | SD |
| 'Rose Irene' | bright rose | SD |
| 'La Jolla' | crimson | SD |
| 'Mme. Landry' | salmon | D |
| 'Mme. Jaulin' | light apple-blossom-pink | SD |
| 'Party Dress' | pale rose-pink | SD |
| 'Salmon Supreme' | medium-light salmon | SD |
| 'Beauté Poitevine' | salmon (usually lighter than 'Salmon Supreme') | SD |
| 'Blaze' | red (darker than 'Irene') | SD |

# 8

# *Miniature, Dwarf, and Semidwarf Geraniums*

Miniature and dwarf (up to three inches tall) geraniums, and semidwarf (up to six inches tall) geraniums, are ideal for people who want to enlarge their collection of geraniums but cannot enlarge their gardening space, and for gardeners who appreciate the diminutive charms of these elfin plants. With dozens of small geraniums to choose from, any gardener can find types to please him.

Among the earliest- and still-listed dwarf geraniums are dark-foliaged red-flowered 'Black Vesuvius,' rose-flowered 'Kleiner Liebling' (Little Darling), single red-flowered 'Mme. Fournier,' and double-red 'Pigmy.'

California hybridizers such as Ernest Rober and David Case carried on the search for small geraniums. Today, Holmes Miller, Los Altos, and William Schmidt, Palo Alto, are among the outstanding West Coast hybridizers.

In the East, Milton Arndt, Hightstown, New Jersey, and Mrs. Bruce Hill, Dalton, Massachusetts, contribute new varieties to the hobbyist's selections of these charming diminutives.

## CULTURE OF THE SMALL ONES

The true miniature geraniums such as dark-leaved salmon-pink flowered 'Imp,' and pink- or red-flowered 'Tiny Tim,' need different handling than the slightly larger types designated as dwarf or semidwarf.

The miniatures are difficult to ship and some dealers will sell them only at the nursery. However, I have had large shipments of these two- or three-inch plants from an Eastern greenhouse without the loss of a single leaf in transit.

Miniatures grow slowly. It is usually safe to leave them in the original pot for several months. Their leaves are small (less than a half-inch wide on 'Tiny Tim'), and they often have a difficult time adjusting to the arid climate of our homes. The experienced indoor gardener will find the miniature geraniums a real challenge, for it is up to him to provide enough humidity to keep foliage and buds of these wee plants from browning and blasting.

When I receive a new group of miniature geraniums for window gardening, I put the little pots on a lazy susan and invert a transparent plastic hatbox over them, providing them with an eight-inch-high miniature greenhouse. The plants are watered and set in a sunny area. When the sides of the hatbox show moisture I lift it for a time, wipe it dry and replace it. If it continues to fog I slip a small piece of wood under each edge to admit air.

Other miniature geraniums are placed directly under fluorescent lights where they thrive. (See Chapter 14.)

If you grow miniature geraniums in a sunny window, assure extra humidity by setting the pots on (or in) moistened gravel or sphagnum moss.

Small plants may lose a few leaves in shipment or begin showing loss of leaves soon after shipment, as do other geraniums. With proper watering, humidity, and light they start new growth in short order.

Keep plants potbound and fertilize only when leaves begin turning lighter green; or, when all other conditions are right and plants fail to flower. Then apply a water-soluble fertilizer at monthly intervals.

Repot when your miniatures have obviously outgrown their containers. This is indicated when new roots show through the bottom of the pot. To transplant, use a soil made of equal parts of clay, garden loam, and sand. If you use the peat moss mixtures (and they are very handy) be prepared for more rapid growth and more frequent repotting.

To repot, knock the plant from the pot and remove algae which may have crusted on the topsoil. Free the roots to some extent by loosening the soil at the top and bottom of the rootball. Plant to their original depth in a pot one size larger. Leave about a half-inch space between pot rim and soil line. Never bury leaves in soil as this may lead to fungus infection or rot.

Water plants thoroughly after repotting, then do not water again until the topsoil feels dry.

Miniatures thrive in the same temperatures recommended for the larger varieties, 65 to 70 degrees during the day with a drop of 10 degrees at night. They must have plenty of light to grow and flower.

## HOW TO DISPLAY DIMINUTIVE GERANIUMS

Small geraniums become lost when mingled with a collection of larger plants, unless they are used as border material.

If you grow plants on a special table, use center and side areas for displaying large geraniums and reserve the edges for the small ones. If those in the front row do not receive enough sun, turn the table around at weekly intervals.

One of my favorite devices for displaying small geraniums is a lazy susan that can be twirled as often as necessary. This is especially nice when you want to emphasize the features of these little charmers to friends who are observing your plant collection.

36. Pelargonium hortorum
'Doc'
PHOTO BY MERRY GARDENS

37. Pelargonium hortorum
*'Emma Hossler'* (*l*). *and*
*'Mr. Everaarts'* (*r.*)
PHOTO BY MERRY GARDENS

38. Pelargonium hortorum
*'Fairy Tales'*
PHOTO BY MERRY GARDENS

39. Pelargonium hortorum
*'Fleurette'*
PHOTO BY MERRY GARDENS

A tea cart also makes an ideal display area; or you may prefer one of the many types of plant stands featured at florists and in department stores.

Another of my favorite ways to display petite plants is in a miniature greenhouse. A crystal-clear dome allows for free vision and controls humidity. This twelve- by twenty-four-inch area houses a dozen diminutive geraniums without crowding.

Of course, small geraniums can be tucked in any sunny spot where you want color or interest.

In a squatty clay strawberry jar I have plantings of large-flowered salmon 'Dancer.' It blooms beautifully for weeks at a time, then rests. But even while resting it makes a pretty picture, for its nicely patterned dark leaves contrast splendidly with the terra-cotta jar.

I like to use decorated jardinieres for displaying some of the prettiest miniature geraniums. Put a few stones in the bottom of a jardiniere before inserting the potted plant. Otherwise water might collect and geraniums do not like to stand in water. If you are fortunate enough to have some large pieces of cholla wood you can make a novel growing area. Enlarge the natural openings in the wood and fill them with well-moistened soil. Anchor the wood upright in a four-inch pot of soil and plant several small geraniums in the wood openings. This is most effective when only one variety is used. Semidwarf 'Emma Hossler' is a splendid choice. It is a fast grower and a free bloomer. When several plants flower along one of the cholla standards the planting looks like a small tree covered with pink and white flowers.

Use the dwarf geraniums in outdoor gardens for borders, in patio container gardens, or in rock gardens. When using them in container gardens try to elevate the containers on steps or boxes, for half the fun of growing these small beauties lies in observing their foliage and flowers.

A few years ago I used a circle of them to top a metal pyramid garden such as is suggested for growing strawberries. I used plants of semidwarf, free-blooming dark salmon 'Fleurette' (it propagates readily) to enhance a display of violas. One of these pyramids would be splendid for summering a complete collection of Lilliputian plants.

Rose-flowered variegated 'Kleiner Liebling' makes a year-round conversation piece in my study. Friends enjoy its white-margined green leaves as much as its rosy flowers.

40. Pelargonium hortorum
'*Kleiner Liebling Variegated*'
PHOTO BY MERRY GARDENS

41. Pelargonium hortorum
'*Red Spider*'
PHOTO BY MERRY GARDENS

42. Pelargonium hortorum
'*Rosy Dawn*'
PHOTO BY MERRY GARDENS

43. Pelargonium hortorum
*'Sneezy'*
PHOTO BY MERRY GARDENS

44. Pelargonium hortorum
*'Snow White'*
PHOTO BY MERRY GARDENS

45. Pelargonium hortorum
*'Tinkerbelle'*
PHOTO BY MERRY GARDENS

46. Pelargonium hortorum
*'Trinket'*
PHOTO BY MERRY GARDENS

# LISTS FOR READY REFERENCE

## Miniature and Dwarf Geraniums

WHITE

'Fairy Tales'
'Milky Way'
'Polaris'
'Small Fortune'

SALMON

'Capella'
'Gypsy Gem'
'Jojo'
'Moonbeam'
'Pride'
'Ruffles'
'Salmon Comet'
'Sprite'
'Tangerine'
'Trinket'
'Tweedle Dum'

ORANGE

'Black Vesuvius'
'Mischief'
'Red Brooks Barnes'
'Rosy Dawn'

SALMON PINK

'Altair'
'Brooks Barnes'
'Filigree'
'Imp'
'Peace'
'Pixie'
'Sirius'

PINK, ROSE

'Alcyone'
'Aldebaran'
'Fairyland'
'Fairy Princess'
'Kiffa'
'Little Trot'
'Tiny Tim'
'Kleiner Liebling'
'Venus'

SCARLET

'Dee Dee'
'Dot'
'Red Comet'
'Saturn'

RED

'Antares'
'Firefly'
'Goblin'
'Jupiter'
'Merope'
'Meteor'
'Perky'
'Pigmy'
'Tiny Tim'
'Volcano'

PURPLE-CRIMSON

'Minx'
'Rocket'

LAVENDER

'Rober's Lavender'

## Semidwarf Geraniums

WHITE

'Delicate'
'Snow White'
'White Emma
    Hossler'

ORANGE

'Black Knight'
'Dancer'
'Orange Galore'

SALMON

'De Witt's Dwarf'
'Fleurette'
'Pride'
'Rober's White with
    Pink Eye'
'Sheratan'
'Talitha'
'Tweedle Dee'

PINK, ROSE

'Dopey'
'Emma Hossler'
'Epsilon'
'Golden Mr.
    Everaarts'

'Little Darling'
'Mr. Everaarts'
'Night and Day'
'Tu-Tone'
'Twinkle'

SCARLET

'Arcturus'
'Brownie'
'Doc'
'Red Spider'
'Sneezy'

RED

'Alpha'
'Red Ridinghood'
'Rober's Dwarf Red'
'Robinhood'
'Scarlett O'Hara'
'Sparkle'

PURPLE-CRIMSON

'Prince Valiant'
'Tempter'

# 9

## *Fancy-leaved Geraniums*

The multicolor splendor of fancy-leaved geraniums triggers the artistic impulse in a gardener. He discovers a color-filled palette from which to "paint" his own garden.

There are such fancy-leaved sorts as 'Verona,' 'Yellow Gem,' and 'Forty-niner,' with foliage drenched in gold. Bronze-leaved varieties 'Jubilee,' 'Alpha,' and 'Maréchal MacMahon' are gold with a bronze zone. There are variegated green-and-white varieties like 'Wilhelm Langguth' and 'Attraction'; bicolored green-and-yellow-leaved plants 'Happy Thought' and 'Crystal Palace Gem'; tricolored leaves of green, brown, and yellow, sometimes splashed with scarlet and purple as in 'Lady Cullum' and 'Skies of Italy'; or double orange-red flowered 'Mrs. Pollock'; and 'Mrs. Cox.' The newer fancies include 'Freak of Nature' with its white leafstalks, thick white leaf-centers, and ruffled green margins; and 'Pistachio' with foliage splashed green, yellow, bronze, and red and leafstalks with streaks of green and white. There are fancy-leaved dwarf geraniums, single- and double-flowered fancy-leaved forms, and even some of the scented-leaved geraniums have fancy leaves.

Many fancy-leaved geraniums originated in England during the Victorian Era of the 1860s, when gold tassels, gilt-edged mirrors, plush scarves, and heavy velvet drapes were preferred. Gardeners were enchanted with the rich beauty of the colored-leaved geraniums.

These same geraniums, and the new forms too, blend or contrast beautifully with modern or traditional decor.

47. Pelargonium hortorum
*'Alpha'*
PHOTO BY MERRY GARDENS

48. Pelargonium hortorum
*'Verona'*
PHOTO BY MERRY GARDENS

49. Pelargonium hortorum
*'Skies of Italy'* (*l.*) *and 'Pink Happy Thought'* (*r.*)
PHOTO BY MERRY GARDENS

50. Pelargonium hortorum
*l. to r., 'Pollock 137,' 'Jubilee,' and 'Miss Burdett Coutts'*
PHOTO BY MERRY GARDENS

51. *Author's plants of*
Pelargonium hortorum
*'Wilhelm Langguth' in strawberry jar.*
PHOTO BY MEL JACOBSEN

52. Pelargonium hortorum
*'Miss Burdett Coutts'*
PHOTO BY MERRY GARDENS

## CULTURE

Culture of the fancy-leaved geraniums approximates that of other garden or *Pelargonium hortorum* types. Foliage color is affected by climatic conditions and light, with brighter colors showing when days are sunny and nights cool. While all varieties need light, some of those with much white and gold in their leaves cannot stand full summer sun. When light is too bright, silver- and gold-leaved and tricolor-leaved geraniums may show cupped-down leaves.

In my indoor gardens, the fancy-leaved geraniums show fine color in east or south placements and in a sunny greenhouse area. Fluorescent-light gardeners will find the steady glow of artificial light brings out depths of color which may be impossible to obtain in window gardens where strong natural light is lacking.

Water when the topsoil feels quite dry to the touch. Fertilize monthly during the growing season, and at all times when leaves start to diminish in size.

Many of the variegated or colored-leaved types are not so strong as green-leaved geraniums, as lack of chlorophyll or green coloring usually weakens the strain. Only six of the vast assortment of "Victorian Varieties" remain on today's lists.

Colored-leaved geraniums are fine bedding or border plants. Assure them of good growing conditions by planting in well-drained areas. If garden soil is heavy clay, lighten it by digging in sand and peat moss.

To plant out, spade holes somewhat larger than the potted plants. Remove the plant from the pot and strike thick lower roots with the tip of a sharp knife. The slight gashes will start roots growing outward rather than in tight spirals. If you garden in arid soil, add a *soil detergent* to the water used to fill the planting hole. Press the rootball into the moist earth, then add enough soil to make a level planting.

One of our prettiest outdoor plantings of fancy-leaved geraniums is around the base of a gas lamp. Creamy yellow old brick edges the planting of salmon-flowered, bronze-and-gold-leaved 'Bronze Beauty.'

A gardening friend mingles plants of pink-flowered, golden-leaved 'Cloth of Gold' with rose-and-pink-flowered *Begonia semperflorens*.

The vigorous growing geranium offers some shade to the lower growing begonias. When both geraniums and begonias are in flower the plantings become mounds of green, pink, and gold.

Silver-, white-, or cream-and-green-leaved geraniums are spectacular when used alone, or they mix happily with other bedding plants and perennials. One of the most effective plantings I have seen was a contrast in form and color of clear yellow snapdragons with the round clusters of double pink-flowered, silver-and-white-leaved geranium 'Hills of Snow.' White alyssum made a lacy border.

White-bordered single red-flowered geranium 'Mountain of Snow' fronted by heaping pots of bright pink dianthus stopped traffic in a container garden. I doubt the Victorians would have used so gaudy a color combination but it was most effective!

I like to use blue flowers with some of the variegated-leaved geraniums. Double pink-flowered, green-and-cream-foliaged geranium 'Mrs. Parker' and twelve-inch mounds of navy-blue delphinium 'Blue Mirror' make a fetching combination.

Well-grown tricolor-leaved geraniums display veritable rainbows on every leaf. If you are interested in tricolors as a collector, and do not plan to work them into the landscape, let your selection be limited only by your space and budget. However, if you plan to use these gayly-colored geraniums with companion plants, choose varieties carefully or you'll have a garden patterned like a crazy quilt!

With foliage of green, rose, brown, and ivory, such as that of 'Miss Burdett Coutts,' it seems almost an anticlimax to find that this fancy-leaved geranium also produces small single scarlet flowers. I like to plant brightly-hued geraniums such as this one and 'Lady Cullum' with silver artemisia, white-flowered annuals such as petunias, snapdragons, alyssum, and silver-blue-leaved, white-flowered *Convolvulus Cneorum.*

In the window garden the fancy-leaved geraniums blend happily with red- or white-flowered *Pelargonium hortorum,* ivy-leaved types, and green- or gray-foliaged scented-leaved geraniums.

Truly magnificent are trees or standards of colored-leaved geraniums. 'Mrs. Cox' and 'Skies of Italy' are adaptable to this form, and are rapid growers. (See Chapter 16.) 'Verona,' a robust grower with pale green-to-gold foliage and pink flowers, also makes an elegant standard.

'Filigree,' a charming fancy originated by Holmes C. Miller, Los Altos, California, is one of the most beautiful of the newer tricolors.

Leaves are silvery green with a wide border of creamy white and lightly zoned with pink and brown. A bushy beauty, it spreads into small mounds dotted with single salmon flowers. Keep 'Filigree' out of direct sun and hot dry winds for its wide white leaf margins burn easily.

The bronze-leaved varieties are extremely handsome when well grown but leaves tend to burn and dry in summer sun, and if grown in too much shade they lose their rich bronze coloring. My bronze-leaved geraniums grow beautifully on our patio where a roof of egg-crate design lets filtered sunlight fall on their leaves. Among the prettiest I have found are the three MacMahons: 'Maréchal Mac-Mahon' with yellow and bronze leaves and single scarlet flowers; 'Magenta MacMahon,' bronze-leaved with single magenta flowers; and 'Pink MacMahon' with bright bronze patterned foliage and pink flowers.

The two 'Alphas' make attractive plants and adapt readily to indoor or outdoor gardening. Semidwarf 'Alpha,' a longtime favorite, has narrow reddish-bronze rings on golden-green leaves. This free-blooming variety has intensely red single flowers. In southern California 'Alpha' blooms profusely even in winter. It is generous with its flowers in our area, too, especially when summered outdoors. Friends from Long Island, New York, say it's "the most floriferous of the fancies." 'Pink Alpha' (Pink Harry Hieover) is a pink-flowered replica of 'Alpha.'

'Black Jubilee' is something very special. When well grown, it displays nearly black leaves topped with dark rosy-salmon flowers. Among the newer varieties this one has moved right up with the top sellers. I have not grown this black beauty yet, but Fred Bode, Jr., recommends it as "superb for arrangements or porch pots and usually a very strong grower."

Other fancy-leaved geraniums are: 'Bronze Beauty,' with yellow-green leaves marked with a rust-red zone and single scarlet flowers. The small bushy plants make fine pot plants.

Rust-red zoning on small, shiny chartreuse green leaves and single salmon flowers characterize 'Golden Oriole.'

'Jubilee' shows broad red-brown zoning on yellow-green leaves. This tall growing plant bears single light salmon flowers.

'Medallion' is a Holmes Miller origination with hairy, shaggy-edged yellow-green leaves centered with big red-brown blotches. Its flowers are small, single, dark salmon.

'Prince Bismarck' shows its single light salmon flowers above medium-large, lobed, yellow-green leaves prettily zoned with shiny rust-red.

The leaves of bicolors, or butterfly geraniums, are exquisitely marked with centers resembling butterflies. 'Happy Thought' has a pretty yellow butterfly in the center of its leaves, green leaf margins, and single red flowers. Although difficult to root, it makes a fine plant once it gets going. 'Pink Happy Thought' is marked the same but has pink flowers. 'Crystal Palace Gem,' one of the oldest of the fancy-leaved geraniums, reverses the pattern and shows a green butterfly in the center, yellow leaf edges and single red flowers.

Plants which fail to flower can be perplexing. Not so with 'Mme. Salleron,' for this six-inch gray-green geranium with white edges has never been known to flower. It makes a pretty border and is splendid in dish gardens.

'Little Trot,' also green with a white edge and small pink flowers (listed as a dwarf), is somewhat larger and less compact than 'Mme. Salleron.' Slow-growing 'Sprite' is another dwarf whose gray-green leaves look as though they have been edged with white frosting. This bushy plant has single salmon-coral flowers.

'Roderick Dhu' cannot properly be classified as dwarf, yet it is somewhat dwarfed in growth. It is not a newcomer, but is regaining popularity because it is a compact grower and is handsomely clothed in yellow foliage with a rust zone, and it makes a marvelous houseplant. When growing conditions are right it produces a bounty of single salmon flowers.

There are some fancy-leaved geraniums which refuse to fall under any definite heading: gold-and-bronze-leaved 'Gold Rush'; red-flowered 'Distinction'; 'Turtle's Surprise' with its colorful white or pink stems supporting green and brown foliage; and heavily-zoned 'Splash' with medium-sized double metallic-salmon flowers.

*Pelargonium frutetorum,* the horseshoe geranium, and its hybrid 'Dark Beauty' have been popular greenhouse geraniums for many years. Two plant breeders have been working with this group creating other colorful-leaved and flowered varieties. Large-growing *P. frutetorum* is marvelous for baskets, banks, or anywhere one wants the advantage of rapid growth and bright flowers. It boasts green leaves with a near-black zone and single salmon flowers. 'Dark Beauty' displays a black center and while it grows to perfection in shade, it can also tolerate sun. In Baja, California, Miss Frances Hartsook has created 'Royal' with zigzagging stems, dark-zoned green leaves, and single salmon flowers.

In Australia the late Ted Both, of amaryllis fame, also produced some new *P. frutetorum* cultivars: 'Magic Lantern,' a topnotch basket plant with brightly-colored red, yellow, and green leaves; and 'Mosaic,' whose dark leaves often show splashings of paler green blending with large salmon flowers.

## PROPAGATING FANCY-LEAVED GERANIUMS

While most cuttings of fancy-leaved cultivars root more slowly than other geraniums, they do root under the same conditions described in Chapter 3. There is one exception: the fancy-leaved geraniums will not tolerate touching one another, especially under confined rooting conditions as in miniature greenhouses or under plastic bags or tents. When propagated this way they often rot before rooting. Space cuttings well apart and if moisture collects on protective covering, remove the covering, wipe it, replace, and provide more adequate ventilation.

Any of the easily grown and propagated fancy-leaved geraniums can be used to fashion stylish and unusual "cutting" trees. (See Chapter 16.)

# 10

## Scented-leaved Geraniums

Scented-leaved geraniums, with multiform foliage, are aromatic mimics of the plant world, impudently copying floral, fruit, nut, spice, and other pungent odors.

Foliage size varies from half-inch lemon-scented *Pelargonium crispum* to four- or five-inch peppermint-scented *P. tomentosum*. Foliage form and texture are of infinite variety: deeply cut as on rose-scented *P. graveolens;* round, ruffled, and smooth in the apple and spice group, *P. fragrans* to *P. odoratissimum;* deeply lobed, toothed, and pungent oak-leaved forms of *P. quercifolium;* fernlike *P. denticulatum* or pine-scented group. The medium-sized foliage of the *P. fulgidum* group includes the best of the flowering scenteds, such as pink-flowered 'Clorinda' and free-flowering red 'Mrs. Taylor.' There is a miscellaneous grouping of coconut, ginger, lime, and southernwood scenteds with foliage and scents different from all others; and there are several scenteds with variegated foliage.

Scenteds make marvelous plants for collectors, for the hobbyist who wants to grow one or two lovely specimen plants, for the arranger who needs something different for her design, or for the gourmet who can turn a commonplace cake into a conversation piece by adding a few rose or lemon geranium leaves to the recipe.

## HISTORY OF THE SCENTEDS

Native to the African Cape, the scented-leaved geraniums were introduced to England about 1632. By the late 1790s scented geraniums were highly fashionable and were widely grown in English castles, cottages, and greenhouses.

Perfume manufacturers became interested in scented-leaved geraniums when they discovered that the rose-scenteds, *Pelargonium radens* and *P. graveolens,* were satisfactory substitutes for expensive rose oils. By 1800 great fields of rose-scented geraniums were being grown in southern France and in Turkey. (Rose-scented geraniums are still grown for perfume in large plantings in Algeria, Spain, Sicily, and France.)

Professional plantsmen profited from the scented geraniums which propagated easily and sold readily. Professional and amateur plant breeders had a carnival with scented-leaved geraniums when they discovered that the plants hybridized easily. Sadly, breeders were careless about recording their work and our taxonomists have found it difficult to classify and reclassify the scenteds.

In 1955 Harold E. Moore, Jr., Bailey Hortorium, Cornell University, published a major work, "Pelargoniums in Cultivation," in *Baileya.* In his work many old favorites are given new names.

## SCENTEDS TO GROW AND SHARE

The scenteds are easy to grow. Give them the same culture as the garden or bedding geraniums. The big ones, such as the peppermint-scented *P. tomentosum* group; 'Snowflake,' the variegated round-leaved rose-scented variety; the neatly-foliaged apple-scented group; and the rough-leaved pungent *P. vitifolium* or grape-leaf geranium; are rapid growers which soon fill the corner of a window garden or a favorite outdoor area.

In our family the apple-scented geranium is a tradition. Each new bride is presented with this smooth-leaved, deliciously scented plant for her new home. The children in the family have improved on the "apple for the teacher" theme by taking to school a small pot of apple-scented geranium. This variety sets seed easily and when grown outdoors its leafy runners make a fragrant ground covering. All summer it is covered with small white flowers dotted red in the throat. In winter it flowers when kept in a cool 65-degree room, but in warmer temperatures buds often blast from heat and lack of humidity. Small plants purchased in the early spring and allowed to grow in the window garden for two or three months before being plunged into the outdoor garden will grow into 18- to 24-inch specimens by fall.

If you want to interest a friend in geraniums, let him rub the leaves of one of the fragrant types. One whiff and he will want to grow them too.

If your growing space is limited you might like to have one plant from each of the eight groups of scenteds; or you could collect all the varieties in the group with the fragrance most appealing to you.

If you must have flowers as well as scented foliage, try some of the *P. fulgidum* group. Not so fragrant as many others, they do have some aroma and most of them have pretty flowers as well.

When purchasing scenteds for the first time, order the truly perfumed kinds such as rose, lemon, or peppermint; or visit a nursery and sniff for yourself—an appealing fragrance is an individual matter.

# EIGHT GROUPS OF SCENTED-LEAVED GERANIUMS

**Rose-scented Group** (*Pelargonium graveolens*). Deeply cut foliage, lavender blooms.

'Attar of Roses,' lobed soft hairy leaf, rich rose perfume
'Dr. Livingston,' deeply cut leaves, lemon-rose scented
'Lady Plymouth,' small variegated foliage
'Little Gem,' pungent, free-flowering
'Red-flowered Rose,' gray-green foliage
'Rober's Lemon Rose,' strongest lemon-rose scent
'Rose,' sweet-scented old favorite
'Snowflake,' round, white-speckled leaf
'Variegated Mint-scented Rose'

**Oak Leaf Group** (*Pelargonium quercifolium*). Showy pink flowers, pungent foliage.

'Fair Ellen,' finest for pots, dark green leaves with brown centers
'Giant Oak,' tall growing, sticky stems, irregular leaves
'Skeleton's Unique,' small ruffled leaves with a dark zone, somewhat trailing in growth habit
'Staghorn Oak,' divided purple-veined leaves, prostrate grower
'Village Hill Oak,' deeply lobed, toothed

53. *Scented-leaved Geranium*
*'Red-flowered Rose'*
PHOTO BY MERRY GARDENS

54. *Scented-leaved Geranium*
*'Little Gem'*
PHOTO BY MERRY GARDENS

55. *Scented-leaved Geranium*
*'Mint-scented Rose'*
PHOTO BY MERRY GARDENS

56. *Scented-leaved Geranium*
   *'Grey Lady Plymouth'*
   PHOTO BY MERRY GARDENS

57. *Scented-leaved Geranium*
   *'Snowflake'*
   PHOTO BY MERRY GARDENS

**Peppermint-scented Group** (*Pelargonium tomentosum*). Large soft leaves covered with densely matted hairs.

'Joy Lucille,' deeply lobed leaf
'Peppermint,' very strong scent
'Pungent Peppermint,' deeply cut leaf

**Pine-scented Group** (*Pelargonium denticulatum*). Pink flowers, deeply cut leaves.

'Apricot,' showy bright pink flowers
*blandfordianum,* gray cut leaf, musk scent, climbing stems
'Crowfoot,' (*P. radens*), deeply cut leaf
*denticulatum,* best fern-leaf type
'Filicifolium,' same as *P. denticulatum*
'Pheasant's Foot,' deeply cut leaf

**Fruit- and Spice-scented Group** (*Pelargonium fragrans* to *P. odoratis-simum*). Trailing, strong scent, small leaves.

'Apple,' ruffled round leaf
'Nutmeg,' silver-gray ruffled leaf
'Old Spice,' apple-and-nutmeg scent

58. *Scented-leaved Geraniums (l. to r.) 'Shrubland Rose,' 'Fair Ellen,' and 'Little Gem'* PHOTO BY MERRY GARDENS

59. *Author's plant of scented-leaved Geranium 'Apple'* PHOTO BY MEL JACOBSEN

**Flowering Group** (*Pelargonium fulgidum*). Medium leaves, showy flowers, mild scents.

'Brilliant,' red flowers
'Clorinda,' showy pink flowers
'Concolor Lace,' red flowers, stronger scent
'Mrs. Kingsley,' red flowers, ruffled leaf
'Mrs. Taylor,' free-blooming red
'Rollinson's Unique,' wine-red flowers
'Scarlet Unique,' gray-green woolly leaves, scarlet flowers with rich black markings on upper petals
'Shrubland Rose,' red flowers

60. *Scented-leaved Geranium 'Mrs. Kingsley'* PHOTO BY MERRY GARDENS

61. *Scented-leaved Geranium 'Scarlet Unique'* PHOTO BY MERRY GARDENS

62. *Scented-leaved Geranium 'Prince of Orange'* PHOTO BY MERRY GAR-DENS

63. *Author's plant of scented-leaved Geranium 'Crispum Minor'* PHOTO
BY MEL JACOBSEN

**Lemon-scented Group** (*Pelargonium crispum*). Leaves small and
ruffled, pink flowers.

'Lemon Crispum' (Finger Bowl), very small leaves
'Crispum Minor,' miniature leaves
'Gooseberry,' leaves mottled yellow
'Lady Mary,' showy pink flowers
'Limoneum,' dark pink flowers
'Orange,' showy flowers, strong scent
'Prince Rupert,' strong, straight, tall, bushy grower
'Prince Rupert Variegated,' leaves margined with creamy white

Take care when watering the lemon-scented geraniums. A slight
amount of overwatering will cause them to wilt and die from bacterial rot.

**Miscellaneous Group**

P. *grossularioides,* coconut-scented, small trailing plant
P. *torento,* ginger-scented, round toothed leaves, lavender flowers
P. *nervosum,* sweet lime scent, serrated leaves, low grower
P. *abrotanifolium,* strong southernwood-scented, finely cut silver leaves, small white flowers, good bonsai or miniature-tree subject

# PROPAGATION

Most cuttings or divisions of the scenteds are easy to root, but there are a few that are difficult. Strawberry-scented *P. Scarboroviae* may stay for weeks in its rooting medium without showing roots. Lift a cutting. If it has a callous or a thickened healed tissue at its base, move it to a pot of fresh soil and it will root in a hurry.

The exquisite 'Prince Rupert Variegated' is difficult for some growers to root. Remove the bottom one-and-one-half inches of foliage from three- to four-inch cuttings, dust with a mixture of one-half talcum powder and one-half rooting hormone powder, and put in rooting medium right up to the leaves. Do not crowd. Give shade and use care in watering. The small cuttings have scant water capacity and need to be watered more often than other cuttings, but this one will not tolerate overwatering.

P. *vitifolium,* the grape-leaf geranium, is a slow rooter, sometimes standing still for five to six months before showing roots.

Dust cuttings about once in ten days with DDT to prevent aphids and white flies.

# DISPLAYING SCENTED-LEAVED GERANIUMS

I like to make specimen plants of my favorite scented geraniums. A plastic-foam pedestal elevates a pot of apple-scented geranium just enough to display its graceful runners. I often place it near a colorful parrot in a glass dome to make an interesting grouping.

Perhaps you will want to copy the whimsical identification markers I use for small scented geraniums. Peppermint is identified with a pipe-cleaner peppermint cane; variegated mint-scented rose displays

64. *Scented-leaved Geranium Grape Leaf* (Pelargonium vitifolium)
PHOTO BY MERRY GARDENS

a peppermint stick centered with a small rose; and strawberry sports a bright red artificial strawberry. You could glue these markers to the pots but I attach them to a florist's pick (a wired pointed stick), let the decoration dangle over the pot edge and secure it by inserting the pointed stick in the soil. A small gingerbread man cut from heavy brown plastic identifies my ginger-scented geranium. Glossy artificial lemons, limes, and oranges add interest to geraniums of corresponding scents.

65. *Author's topiary tree of scented-leaved geraniums.* PHOTO BY MEL JACOBSEN

66. *Plastic ball from toy counter, filled with growing medium treated with soil detergent, forms topiary base.* PHOTO BY MEL JACOBSEN

It is easy to make a pretty topiary tree or holiday hanging from cuttings of scented geraniums. Both make thoughtful, inexpensive gifts. Cover a topiary tree with fruit- or spice-scented cuttings. An attractive hanging ball filled with fragrant cuttings and topped with a red or a green ribbon makes a gala holiday decoration—the idea is the same as the old pomander balls made by sticking cloves in oranges. To make pelargonium pomanders, form moist sphagnum moss or a mixture of moss, peat moss, and perlite into a small ball. Cover it with chicken wire or aluminum foil. Insert cuttings in the moist rooting medium. Add a wire or ribbon to suspend it, and you've made a living pomander ball.

For the base of pelargonium pomanders or scented topiary trees I use toy plastic balls which I purchase at a variety store. The balls have round or horizontal openings. Spray the ball green, red, gold, or silver. Fill it with growing medium which has been treated with soil detergent, then insert the cuttings through the openings in the ball. When treated with soil detergent the balls do not need further watering for several days.

Use calloused or slightly-rooted cuttings in the balls. When the planting is finished, cover it lightly with a ventilated piece of plastic to keep leaves firm, for some of the scenteds, particularly rose and mint, wilt easily. Remove the plastic after the fourth or fifth day. The strawberry-scented geranium is fine for this as it roots slowly. Immerse the ball in water for a few minutes. Let it drain over a large-mouthed fruit jar or vase.

Make a topiary tree of small-leaved lemon-scented geraniums. (See Chapter 16.) Finish it with a flourish by adding several small artificial lemons purchased at your florist's or variety store.

Display scented geraniums in strawberry jars or on an early American spice shelf.

Mingle the scented geraniums with other fragrant potted plants. I can think of no lovelier combination than my fragrant gardenia and my mint-scented pelargonium.

When my potted lemons, oranges, and limes are flowering, I like to place near them the pelargoniums of the same scent. Gardeners enjoy comparing the scents of the citrus plants with those of the geraniums.

Trailing *Plectranthus australis* and miniature roses are marvelous companion plants for any of the rose-scented geraniums. When the air is warm the plectranthus gives off a delightful odor of rose talcum powder, and the miniature roses have a true rose scent.

## BONUSES FROM SCENTED-LEAVED GERANIUMS

Slip a scented leaf in letters to friends.

Dry scented leaves, mix with orrisroot, tie in squares of filmy material with a pretty ribbon, and you have a charming sachet to use or give away.

When making apple jelly place a leaf of rose-scented geranium in the bottom of the glass to give the jelly a piquant flavor.

Rose geranium leaves placed under baking apples or pears impart a new flavor to the fruit.

Leaves of *P. crispum* are often used in finger bowls—the plant is commonly called the finger-bowl geranium.

Place a few leaves of lemon- or rose-scented geraniums in the bottom of a lightly greased cake pan, pour the cake mixture over the leaves and bake. The mixture may come prepared, but it will have a gourmet flavor when it is baked.

Crush leaves of rose-, lemon-, and peppermint-scented geraniums. Cover with boiling water and steep for thirty minutes. Drain the liquid and use it as part of the water for making iced tea.

Garnish iced tea with a leaf of lemon-scented geranium. Garnish iced coffee with a leaf of peppermint-scented geranium.

To make a potpourri of long-lasting color and fragrance, use petals from newly opened roses, highly scented geranium leaves, and petals from some of your brightest salmon-colored geraniums for color. Dry petals and leaves on a rack out of the sun, permitting the air to circulate among them. Spread the petals thinly so they will not mold. Dry them until they are as crisp as cornflakes. Limp petals mold in jars.

You will need fixatives such as orrisroot and gum benzoin, which you can buy at the drugstore or from an herb specialist. It takes one-and-one-half gallons of fresh petals and leaves to make a pint of dried material. When dry mix well in a large vessel and place in airtight jars. The fragrance of the mixture improves as it ages.

Here is a basic recipe that can be varied with dried orange peel stuck with cloves, a few drops of orange flower oil, and a few drops of rose oil:

*2 quarts dried rose petals*
*1 pint dried rosebuds*
*½ pint dried lavender flowers*
*1 quart dried rose geranium leaves*
*1 pint dried lemon-scented geranium leaves and/or lemon verbena*
*1 cup chopped orrisroot*
*½ cup gum benzoin tears* (*crumbs*)
*1 cup rosemary leaves*

# 11

# Trailing and Climbing
# Ivy-leaved Geraniums

*Pelargonium peltatum,* the ivy geranium, is so named because its leaves are peltate, or shield-shaped. The stem is attached to the lower surface of the leaf instead of at the base or margin.

In this group of geraniums are trailing, twining, and vining treasures that beautify indoor gardens, patios, and landscapes. In California they are often sold in flats to be used as ground covers. We use them in hanging baskets, on totems, trellises, or in elevated pots to grace pillars and posts, or as ground cover near a pool.

The ancestors of this group have long since vanished, but the descendants are many. Flower colors range from white to red and the foliage may be plain or variegated green-and-white, or white, cream, pink, and green as on 'Sunset' (L'Élégante).

## CULTURE OF IVY-LEAVED GERANIUMS

The ivy-leaved geraniums are sun worshipers and grow best when they receive full sun. In California I saw unshaded lawns and banks covered with these lovely plants. They are used instead of grass in private and public gardens.

Culture of the ivy-leaved geraniums is the same as that for *Pelargonium hortorum,* the garden geraniums. Tip cuttings of these obliging plants root quickly in water and can, indeed, be grown for weeks in a container of water.

Take cuttings in the fall. For a strong bushy plant pinch out the tip as soon as the cutting is rooted. In four to six weeks the cutting

67. *Ivy-leaved Geranium 'Sunset'* ('L'Élégante') PHOTO BY MERRY GAR-
DENS

should be ready to plant in a three- to five-inch pot. For a real
specimen plant, shift it in five to six months to a six-inch pot of
good soil. Remove the new shoots as they appear above the flower
buds to send full strength into the flower head and you will have a
stunning plant. For a big plant in a hurry, plant three cuttings in
a six-inch pot or five cuttings in a twelve-inch basket.

The ivy-leagued varieties grow more rapidly than any of the other
geraniums. Fertilize them at monthly intervals. A week after fertilizing you should see two-inch growths of fresh green leaves.

Bacterial rot may occur if plants receive too much heat and
humidity. Indoors, ivy-leaved geraniums flower best in a cool 55- to
60-degree room. But many of mine send out small flower clusters
under less desirable conditions, such as daytime temperatures in the
70s if the night temperature is dropped by five to ten degrees.

Water when topsoil feels dry to the touch. The foliage of the variegated 'Sunset' becomes a distinctly shocking bright pink when the plant is allowed to become dry, and returns to white, cream, and green variegation when it is watered. It will tolerate this somewhat abusive treatment almost endlessly.

## DISPLAYING IVY-LEAVED GERANIUMS

Ivy-leaved geraniums are grown as easily as philodendrons, and certainly more easily than many types of true ivy.

A basket with double rose-flowered 'Charles Turner' barely trailing over the sides was hung on our patio in May. It finished the season with four- and five-foot trailers of green leaves colored with dozens of rosy flower clusters.

Try semidouble blood-red 'Mexican Beauty' in a white pot placed atop a white post, or indoors on a sunny mantel or pedestal.

Train double-flowering blue-lavender 'Santa Paula' on a totem pole just as though it were philodendron or ivy.

Double-flowering purple 'Joseph Warren' interplanted with double medium-pink 'Galilee' makes a striking trellis planting.

Ivy-leaved geraniums can be trained on intricate forms such as wire cascades, wire-formed birds, and wreaths or trees made from strong wire or bent coat hangers.

One of my ivy-leaved plantings that never fails to elicit comments grows in a 14-inch length of cholla wood. The wood is used upright, as the trunk of a tree, with the trailing geranium dropping in fountain-like sprays from the top.

To make such a tree, take ivy-leaved geranium cuttings in July or August. Soak a piece of cholla wood in soil detergent solution for a few minutes. Wedge one end of the cholla wood tightly in a small pot. Place a layer of pot chips in the bottom of a larger container, set the pot with the cholla wood on the chips, and fill the space between the two pots with light friable soil which contains at least one-third peat moss. Stuff the openings in the cholla wood with moistened soil. Fibers running across the openings help keep the soil from falling out. Cover the wood with foil or plastic for a few days or until the soil compacts and stays in without the covering. Plant the rooted cuttings in the pockets of soil. Roots will travel the length of the wood and fill the container. Fertilize sparingly as lush growth is not desirable in these plantings. When the planting

68. *Ivy-leaved Geranium 'Mexican Beauty'* PHOTO BY MERRY GARDENS

69. *Ivy-leaved Geranium 'New Dawn' has double rose-cerise flowers.* PHOTO BY MERRY GARDENS

70. *Ivy-leaved Geranium 'Santa Paula'* PHOTO BY MERRY GARDENS

becomes potbound, it can be shifted to a larger container, cholla wood and all.

For unusual effects, plant harmonizing or contrasting ivy-leaved geraniums in a cholla wood trunk. Double medium-red 'Carlos Uhden' and double 'Lilac White' make a nice contrast. Double lavender-blue 'Santa Paula' and double violet-purple 'Joseph Warren' harmonize beautifully.

Sculptured topiary trees can be managed easily with ivy-leaved geraniums. Start with a small plant and train it; or, for faster results, select one with long trailing growth and reshape it to a topiary.

The foundation of the topiary tree is a plastic-foam ball anchored on a dowel. The size will be determined by the plants. I like to use a ball six inches in diameter and an 18-inch wooden dowel one-half inch in diameter. Drill half-inch holes to a one-inch depth in the center bottom and top of the ball. Cut a wooden disk to fit the inside bottom of a six-inch pot. Drill a half-inch diameter hole in the center of the disk. Insert the dowel in the hole in the disk and fasten the plastic-foam ball to the top of the dowel. (I add some waterproof glue to hold the dowel and ball together.) Select an ivy-leaved geranium of strong growth which is ready to be shifted to a six-inch pot. Place one-half inch of pot chips on top of the wooden disk and around the bottom of the dowel, add soil, and plant the geranium. A three- or four-foot-long plant with a single trunk gives the prettier effect, but three or four shorter stems may be used. Strip the leaves from the bottom four-to-five-inches of trunk. Tie the trunk to the dowel with inconspicuous plastic ties or moss-green bias tape. Train the stems around the ball, beginning at its base. Use wreath pins or paper-clip halves as small staples to fasten the stems and leaves to the ball. Press the clips over, not through, the plant material.

As the plant matures continue training it to cling to the ball. If it grows too large for the single ball, add a topknot (another smaller ball) or perhaps a spire. Bend the plant gently, for older stems may break. If a stem splinters during training pull it together with an adhesive bandage or clear cellophane tape. Color the bandage strip gray-green and it will never be noticed among the leaves. When blossoms appear bend them gently, too. A flowering ivy-leaved geranium trained in this fashion looks like a small topiary rose tree in flower. The handsomely variegated 'Sunset' make an exquisite topiary.

71. *Author's ivy-leaved geranium grown on cholla wood.* PHOTO BY MEL JACOBSEN

72. *Author wrapped cholla wood with aluminum foil until the geranium roots became established.* PHOTO BY MEL JACOBSEN

73. *Author's topiary tree, trained from ordinary plant of ivy-leaved geranium.* PHOTO BY MEL JACOBSEN.

# VARIETIES OF IVY-LEAVED GERANIUMS

Specialist geranium growers list many ivy-leaved varieties which are available by mail. Your local greenhouse or nursery may have one or more of these ten favorites:

'Apricot Queen,' double salmon-pink, centers age to white, medium trailing.

'Carlos Uhden,' double bright red flowers with white center, medium trailing.

'Charles Monselet,' large double cerise-red flowers, compact trailing.

'Charles Turner,' double rose-pink flowers, strong growing, long trailing.

'Double Lilac White,' double white flowers sometimes showing lilac center, medium trailing.

'Galilee,' double light clear pink flowers, free blooming, medium trailing.

'Joseph Warren,' double flowers of clear violet-purple, compact trailing.

'Mexican Beauty,' semidouble intense dark blood-red flowers, free blooming, long trailing.

'Salmon,' semidouble clear salmon flowers with reddish veining, long trailing.

'Santa Paula,' double lavender-blue flowers, free blooming, long trailing.

Ivy-leaved geraniums have been crossed with zonal geraniums to produce such fine pot and basket plants as double orchid-pink cerise-blotched 'Alliance.' 'Irma,' with small double salmon-apricot flowers centered with white, is a real beauty with a color not found in any other geranium. 'Scarlet Beauty' has vivid double-scarlet flowers. And if you want really large flowers, try 'E. H. Trego.' Not so vine-like as most ivy-leaved geraniums, it bears enormous double flowers of intense red.

In addition to 'Sunset,' there are other variegated ivy-leaved geraniums. In California I saw three Australian creations: 'Aureum marginatum,' yellow leaves marked with brown and single pink flowers; 'Crocodile,' shiny leaves with creamy white veining and single dark-rose flowers; 'White Mesh,' light mesh-patterned foliage and semidouble pink flowers.

# 12

## *Lady Washington Pelargoniums*

The Lady Washington pelargoniums are the ballerinas of the Geranium family. They are known as Regal, Fancy, Show, Royal, and Martha Washington geraniums. Botanically all are varieties of *Pelargonium domesticum*. Dealers usually accord these plants the dignity of listing them as pelargoniums.

Many of the varieties have been created in the United States. An 1847 variety was given the name of the first lady, Martha Washington. The name was simplified to Lady Washington and applied to any and all plants of *P. domesticum* derivation. Dealers have lately returned to listing these beautiful plants as regals, as they were listed until 1910.

Perhaps you recognize the Lady Washingtons as the lovely gift plants usually displayed during May. The azalea-, petunia- or pansy-like flowers are often rose, or lavender with upper petals marked with dark purple. Specialists list regals with flowers of white, pink, lavender, purple, rose, red, bronze, or near-black satin-textured petals overlaid with golden or smoky tones. They grow in single- and double-flowering forms. A California dealer reports that new varieties such as red-veined ruffled-lavender 'Confetti' and dark-blotched white 'Aztec' surpass older varieties so fast that more than half the varieties listed five years ago have been dropped and half of today's favorites were not on sale ten years ago.

No species of *Pelargonium domesticum* are known to be in cultivation now. The earliest hybrids are thought to have been the progeny of *P. cucullatum,* a shrubby plant with red flowers, and perhaps *P. angulosum* with "rigid angled leaves" covered with "harsh

74. *Lady Washington Geranium*
*'African Belle'*
PHOTO BY MERRY GARDENS

75. *Lady Washington Geranium*
*'Bimbo'*
PHOTO BY MERRY GARDENS

76. *Lady Washington Geranium*
*'Black Lace'*
PHOTO BY MERRY GARDENS

77. *Lady Washington Geranium*
*'Chicago Market'*
PHOTO BY MERRY GARDENS

78. *Lady Washington Geranium*
*'Chorus Girl'*
PHOTO BY MERRY GARDENS

79. *Lady Washington Geranium*
*'Dubonnet'*
PHOTO BY MERRY GARDENS

hair." Derivatives of these species were known in England in 1690. The German breeders Faiss, Richter, and Burgers transformed the small purple-, rose-and-white pansy geranium, 'Mrs. Layal,' into large colorful varieties such as 'Grossmama Fischer,' 'Spring Magic,' and 'Marie Vogel.' These varieties were such vast improvements that even today some of them appear on lists of favorite pelargoniums sent to me by more than one hundred hobbyists.

## THE REGALS OF TODAY

Hybridizers continue to breed for bigger, better, longer-blooming regals. William E. Schmidt, Palo Alto, California, has introduced many delightful varieties. 'Grand Slam,' the most popular regal in this country, is his 1950 introduction. This compact, early blooming rose-red free-flowering variety has large ruffled flowers and is one of the finest red-flowered regals grown.

Other handsome hybrids created by Mr. Schmidt are pale orchid plum-blotched 'Amour'; melon-pink 'Gibson Girl' with black-blotched petals; and 'Black Magic,' whose black buds open to large red-black flowers. 'Parisienne,' a repeating bloomer, displays masses of deep mauve flowers with white centers. 'Rapture' is rich apricot-pink and makes a marvelous pot plant, blooming again and again under favorable conditions.

In California most regal geraniums start blooming the latter part of May and flower well into July. In early June I saw hundreds of gorgeous plants in startling new colors and delightful forms while visiting Clara and Harry May in Long Beach. Working on an average-sized city lot with a small greenhouse, a shaded patio and lathhouse combination, and many cold frames, the Mays carry on an extensive regal geranium hybridizing program. Many of the top thirty varieties are their introductions.

'Vin Rouge' has frilly deep-red flowers with a scarlet overlay. 'Halo' has double golden-salmon flowers with small dark markings and a smoky-plum edging. The white-centered flowers of 'Strawberry Sundae' are the luscious color of fresh strawberries mashed into cream. 'Confetti' flowers do not waterspot as do some varieties; the plant just gets prettier, and it has five distinct flowering cycles. 'Dark Venus' is purple-red when grown in a bright location but in the Mays' patio lath-house where it received some shade it showed

80. *Lady Washington Geranium 'Empress of Russia'* PHOTO BY MERRY GARDENS

81. *Lady Washington Geranium 'Grand Slam'* PHOTO BY MERRY GARDENS

huge red flowers overlaid with shimmering brown. 'Black Top' is a strong grower with a long blooming season. Its two upper petals are black, the lower petals vivid red.

Fred Bode, Jr., Escondido, California, has introduced many regal hybrids. 'White Sails' has pure white flowers showing light veining in the throat; and 'Melissa' is a free-blooming strawberry-pink that makes a fine basket or pot plant. According to Mr. Bode, 'Pink Conspicuous' should bloom easily anywhere. 'Caprice' provides marvelous long-stemmed bright rose-pink flowers for cutting. 'Red Copper,' rose-red flowers with salmon sheen, is fine for baskets as it grows rangy with age. Plants of 'Firedancer' become completely clothed in ruffled crimson flowers—the side growth blooms as heavily as the top growth.

Miss Frances Hartsook, a professional plant breeder, Baja, California, has developed some interesting new cultivars using 'Scarlet Unique,' a scented-leaved geranium of the *P. fulgidum* group, as one parent and various regal geraniums as the other parent. Of bushy growth, the new cultivars have flowers about three-quarters the size of the regal flowers, the continuous blooming habit of 'Scarlet Unique,' and scented leaves. 'Hula' has bright salmon flowers; 'Carefree' has bright crimson-red flowers; 'Mystery' bears masses of deep red-and-black flowers.

Other active breeders of regal geraniums are Kerrigan, Horner, Outwater, Brown, Evan, and Reeves.

## CULTURE OF REGAL GERANIUMS

The regal geraniums, with their stiff rounded leaves and flowers that imitate azaleas, petunias, and pansies, bear little resemblance to any of the other geraniums. They differ in culture, too.

In winter they need to be grown in cool 40- to 50-degree temperatures. At 60 degrees leaf margins may brown. I hold some of mine over the winter in a section of my small greenhouse, and a few older, larger plants are carried over in the south windows of a vacant bedroom. Water when the topsoil feels dry and spray the foliage with a houseplant bomb once a week to discourage white flies.

Move the plants outdoors for summer. Mine go into the garden the first week in June. In some areas of California they can re-

82. *Lady Washington Geranium* '*Mrs. Layal*' PHOTO BY MERRY GARDENS

83. *Lady Washington Geranium 'Waltz Time'* PHOTO BY MERRY GARDENS

main in the ground all year. Friends in Virginia and South Carolina winter their regals as I do.

Fertilize monthly during the summer. Take cuttings in late July and August for starting new plants. Move plants indoors before frost. Prune them back to three or five inches, depending on lower leaf growth. Completely denuded stalks may die if trimmed too severely. It is a good policy to leave no more than three or four growing stems. I like to maintain some of mine as single-stemmed plants. I use a pair to flank our living-room entryway in summer, and to add special interest to patio plantings.

Stems of regal geraniums are tough and woody. If one happens to splinter from the wind or from a small dog jumping into it, as mine has done, support the broken section with a heavy pot label or piece of wood tied to the trunk. Dress the wound with grafting wax if available. The break will heal and the plant will be almost as strong as it was before the damage.

Transplant regal geraniums when they get too large for their pots, usually every second year. If you have no space for larger pots, trim off the excess root growth which may be showing outside the present pot, scrape away an inch of topsoil and replace it with fresh soil.

When regals are resting, they should be watered lightly, about once a week. To bring them into spring and summer bloom, move the plants to a 60-degree growing area early in February and begin the fertilizing program. If white flies appear, spray the foliage with a houseplant bomb.

The plants should be heavily budded and showing color by Easter and ready for the outdoor garden in May or when your garden is frost-free.

Use the Lady Washington geraniums where you want rich color: as specimen plants, in beds, borders, or sunny foundation plantings.

Two- to four-inch cuttings taken in August and potted in two-and-one-half inch pots of nonorganic medium or a mixture of equal parts sand, soil, and peat moss, root in four to five weeks in home conditions. In the greenhouse they may root in two weeks.

As they mature shift to four-inch pots of your favorite growing mixture. (See Chapter 2.) Keep plants compact by pinching out tips in November and December. Many will flower in the four-inch pots, but if they need another transplanting, shift them to six-inch pots before moving them outdoors in spring.

Some pelargoniums grow tall and shrubby with age. They can be kept in bounds by cutting back before bringing them in for winter rest.

Small plants shipped by specialists grow rapidly and usually flower the first season.

# 13

## *Geraniums for Collectors*

That special breed of gardener, the collector of ornamental plants, can satisfy his most exquisite tastes and discriminating specifications in the Geranium family of plants.

His goal may be the grand one of locating and obtaining the world's best zonal geraniums; or his taste may be so delicately honed that he can tolerate only the novel bird's-egg geraniums. A gardener with a botanical inquisitiveness is satisfied by collecting the rare species pelargoniums. A hobbyist to whom fragrance is a required dividend will search high, low, and yonder for new scented-leaved geraniums. A gardener restricted in his enthusiasms by limited space may decide that he cannot provide room and board for any plant more than six inches tall, and he searches endlessly for the miniature, dwarf and semidwarf geraniums. The serenity of the trailing and climbing ivy-leaved geraniums satisfies the need of a gardener who has a hectic daily occupation. The soul of another gardener exults in color, and the variegations of the fancy-leaved geraniums gratify him greatly. A gardener whose byword is beauty may confine himself to the regal or Lady Washington pelargoniums. The collector who must have what nobody else has assembles the rare, unusual, and odd geraniums.

The place to find a good selection of collectors' items is in the catalogs and lists of the specialist geranium growers who sell by mail. The names and addresses of these sources of choice geraniums are listed in Chapter 20. Described here are some of the fascinating plants you can order:

**Rosebud Geraniums.** For the connoisseur who appreciates the delicate beauty of extremely double tiny rosettes which never open wide, resembling clusters of miniature half-opened roses. Budded cuttings taken in early fall usually continue growing into pretty flowering plants. Ceramic or glazed pots are nice foils for these plants. The pink and scarlet flowers can be candied in syrup for dessert decorations.

'Apple Blossom,' a spring symphony of sparkling white flowers with rose-red edges. The firm, long-lasting flowers are perfect for corsages and arrangements. My neighbor plants masses of this geranium along the foundation of her white colonial house.

'Cook's Scarlet & White Rosebud,' brilliant scarlet petals with nearly-white reverse side.

'Magenta Rosebud,' really cerise-red rather than magenta; reddish-lavender crockery makes a colorful container.

'Pink Rosebud,' actually light rose-red flowers with lighter reverse.

'Scarlet Rosebud,' brilliant scarlet flowers, beautiful when planted in a moss-green container.

**Cactus- or Poinsettia-flowered Geraniums.** Petals are long and slender, sometimes straight and sometimes twisted and rolled. The plants bloom readily indoors. Large, old plants are impressive, but smaller, space-saving plants can be started each year from cuttings.

'Hulda Conn,' double salmon flowers.

'Mischief,' a Holmes Miller dwarf geranium, double orange-scarlet blooms.

'More Mischief,' another Holmes Miller dwarf, double pale-shrimp flower petals penciled deep salmon.

'Morning Star,' soft double salmon flowers.

'Noel,' double pure white flowers.

'Pink Poinsettia,' soft rose-pink flowers.

'Poinsettia,' double brilliant red flowers.

'Puff,' graceful umbels of well-spaced double white flowers.

'Red Spider,' narrow, tightly-rolled, rich scarlet petals; fine dark green leaves; semidwarf plant.

'Silver Stars,' large single pure white flowers.

'Southern Cross,' large double coral-red flowers, free flowering. A cutting started in July was budded when Ginger the cat tipped it over. It budded again, and a glass shelf above it broke and severed the buds. In spite of these discouragements, it was in flower by January.

'Starlet,' double, glowing rose-salmon flowers.

84. *Rosebud Geranium 'Apple Blossom'* PHOTO BY MERRY GARDENS

85. *Cactus- or Poinsettia-flowered Geranium 'Noel'* PHOTO BY MERRY GARDENS

'Star of Persia,' double, deep crimson-purple flowers, pointed, slightly twisted petals.

**Carnation-flowered Geraniums.** Notched, serrated, or pinked petal edges resembling carnations or pinks.

'Cerise Carnation,' large double cerise flowers borne in great clusters; plant looks like a bouquet of carnations.

'Jeanne,' sharply serrated single salmon flowers borne in full clusters; free-flowering; bushy. Sometimes listed as 'Sweet William.'

'Mme. Thibaut,' single carnation-like flowers, white with red veins; the small flowers turn pink as they age.

**Bird's-egg Geraniums.** Petals speckled with tiny carmine dots, like a bird's egg. Very free-blooming.

'Double Lavender Pink,' orchid-pink flowers with white centers, petals speckled with rose-red dots.

86. *'White Bird's-egg' Geranium has white flowers dotted rosy red.*
PHOTO BY MERRY GARDENS

'Mrs. J. J. Knight,' pale pink flowers with rose dots, free-flowering, slow-growing.

'Single Cerise,' beautiful cerise flowers but the speckles do not show up well.

'Single Coral,' large coral flowers with rose dots.

'Single Light Pink,' white-centered pink flowers with rose dots.

'Single Rose Pink,' fine flower, good speckles.

### Other Unusual and Odd Geraniums.

'New Life,' double red-and-white twisted florets in abundance on a low bushy plant. Also known as 'Flag of Denmark' and 'Stars and Stripes.'

'Single New Life,' individual flowers may be red flecked with white, plain red, or white with pink phlox eye, or all three on the same plant. Also known as 'Peppermint Stick.'

87. *'Mr. Wren' Geranium* PHOTO BY MERRY GARDENS

'Mr. Wren,' single scarlet flowers with white edge. Petals look as though the red had been painted on in three or four narrow brushstrokes, each ending at a different length on the white.
'Fraîcheur,' double white flowers with narrow margin of red.
'Will Rogers,' very large vivid purple-crimson flowers.
'Dahlia Flowered,' double clear scarlet-red flowers the size of a fifty-cent piece, each with thirty-five small petals with white eye.
'Phlox,' single flowers, white on very light pink, with half of each floret bright pink or very light red.
'Carmel,' picotee single white flowers with narrow margin of bright red.

## RARE SPECIES PELARGONIUMS

*P. acetosum.* Nicely-formed small gray-green succulent leaves, light salmon flowers, thin stems. Leaves shaped somewhat like those of ivy-leaved geraniums, have the flavor of wild sorrel and can be used in salads.

*P. acerifolium.* Large bushy plant, hairy gray three- to five-lobed leaves, purple flowers streaked with darker purple, believed to be an ancestor of present-day Lady Washington pelargoniums.

*P.* x *ardens.* Graceful sprays of single scarlet flowers marked with glowing mahogany rise from dark green basal leaves. Several growers of *P.* x *ardens* have reported that hummingbirds nest in the plants.

88. Pelargonium dasycaule PHOTO BY MERRY GARDENS

89. Pelargonium formosum PHOTO BY MERRY GARDENS

*P. Burtoniae*. Upright plant with small round leaves and slender-petaled coral flowers.

*P. carnosum*. Succulent, wide, cut leaves which are rue-scented, cream-colored flowers.

*P. cordifolium*. Violet-leaved, lavender-flowered, mildly scented.

*P. corianderifolium*. Trailing branches of threadlike foliage, beautiful basket plant.

*P. dasycaule*. Deeply cut leaves, fleshy stems and branches; narrow-petaled creamy flowers are red-spotted.

*P.* x *divaricatum*. The absinthe geranium, feathery gray-green foliage, small single rose flowers. Good subject for bonsai culture.

*P. echinatum*. The sweetheart geranium. Spiny stems, heart-shaped maroon markings on white flowers. In Pasadena, California, I saw a magnificent specimen growing in a cactus and succulent garden.

*P. ferulaceum*. Succulent, finely cut leaves; paper-white flowers.

90. Pelargonium fulgidum PHOTO BY MERRY GARDENS

*P. formosum.* The fingered, or five-fingered geranium. Upright-growing, medium-sized leaves cut into three main sections and five or more secondary sections. Long stems carry as many as fifty semi-double white-tipped salmon flowers per cluster. Flowers the year around with good care. Grow with slight shade. Taxonomists doubt that *P. formosum* is the correct name of this plant, and its origin is not definitely known, but it is a fine collector's item.

*P. fulgidum.* Celandine-leaved storksbill. Plush leaves, vivid scarlet flowers. Does not branch when it is cut back. Mrs. Harry May, Long Beach, California, reports that it is almost impossible to obtain a bushy plant—new plants grow from the cutting scars.

*P. gibbosum.* Knotted storksbill. Climbing plant with small yellow flowers which are fragrant.

*P. x glaucifolium.* Deep maroon and gold flowers fragrant in the evening.

91. Pelargonium gibbosum PHOTO BY MERRY GARDENS

*P. ranunculophyllum.* Tuberous-rooted, dainty hairy leaves with and without zoning, yellow flowers. Germinates readily from seed and grows rapidly. The name is in doubt.

*P. rapaceum.* Tuberous-rooted, soft ferny foliage, clusters of small yellow sweet pea-like flowers. Hard to find; some collectors have obtained seed from South Africa.

*P. reniforme.* Soft furry gray leaves, slender stems, single bright

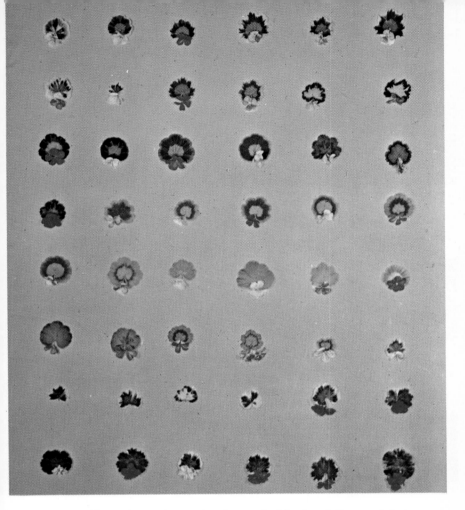

[8]. *Fancy-leaved geraniums, showing typical leaf and flower of forty-eight named varieties. Beginning at top, left to right, Row 1: 'Carlton's Velma,' 'Mrs. Henry Cox,' 'Contrast,' 'Single Pollock,' 'Double Pollock,' and 'Skies of Italy.' Row 2: 'Miss Burdett Coutts,' 'Pastel,' 'Lady Cullum,' 'Pollock 137,' 'Pink Happy Thought,' and 'Red Happy Thought.' Row 3: 'Pistachio,' 'Black Diamond,' 'Red Black Diamond,' 'Jubilee,' 'Dark Beauty,' and 'Distinction.' Row 4: 'Lady Luck,' 'Medallion,' 'Prince Bismarck,' 'Bronze Beauty No. 1,' 'Bronze Beauty No. 2,' and 'Maréchal MacMahon.' Row 5: 'Pink MacMahon,' 'Damon's Gold Leaf,' 'Golden MacMahon,' 'Verona,' 'Dwarf Gold Leaf,' and 'Cloth of Gold.' Row 6: 'Forty-niner,' 'Crystal Palace Gem,' 'Alpha,' 'Green Gold,' 'Golden Oriole,' and 'Filigree.' Row 7: 'Mme. Salleron,' 'Little Trot,' 'Freak of Nature,' 'Mountain of Snow,' 'Flowers of Spring,' and 'Silver S. A. Nutt.' Row 8: 'Hills of Snow,' 'Silver Ruby,' 'Mrs. Parker,' 'Wilhelm Langguth,' 'Attraction,' and 'Beckwiths Pride.'* PHOTO BY MERRY GARDENS

*Hybrid Lady Washington geraniums* (Pelargonium domesticum) *from Clara and Harry May, Long Beach, California.* PHOTOS BY MAY

[9].
'Grand Opera'

[10].
'Minuet'

[11].
'Vin Rouge'

[12].
'Dark Venus'

[13].
'Red Chiffon'

[14].
'Jessica May'

[15].
'Halo'

[16].
'Chorus Girl'

[17].
'King Midas'

[18].
'Confetti'

[19].
'Roulette'

[20].
'Strawberry Sundae'

92. Pelargonium *x* rutaceum PHOTO BY MERRY GARDENS

purple-rose flowers on long peduncles. The flowers are fine material for floral arrangements.

*P.* x *rutaceum.* Tuberous-rooted, ferny gray-green leaves, small maroon flowers, evening scent of rue.

*P. salmoneum.* Small round leaves, round-petaled salmon flowers.

*P. scabrum.* Tall, woody plant, divided rough foliage, small lavender and purple penciled flowers.

93. Pelargonium salmoneum PHOTO BY MERRY GARDENS

94. Pelargonium scandens PHOTO BY MERRY GARDENS

95. Pelargonium *x* Stapletonii PHOTO BY MERRY GARDENS

*P. scandens.* Round, glossy dark green leaves, clusters of narrow petaled single magenta flowers. A climber good on a trellis.

*P.* x *Stapletonii.* Red sweetheart geranium. Spiny-stemmed cactus type, lovely reddish-pink flowers, petals marked with deep purple.

*P. tabulare.* No description and the name is in doubt. The plant is native to Kirstenbosch, South Africa. I am growing seedlings

96. Pelargonium tetragonum PHOTO BY MERRY GARDENS

given to me by a friend—anticipation and surprise are among the joys of collecting geraniums.

*P. tetragonum.* Jenkinsonia cranesbill. Square-stalked, unequal three- and four-sided stalks, small rounded fleshy leaves, four-petaled rose-and-white flowers, orchid-like in form. Fine basket plant, rapid grower.

# 14

## *Growing Geraniums with Artificial Light*

When you collect geraniums and grow them from seed and cuttings, indoor gardening space with good natural light appears to shrink rapidly! Let electricity come to your rescue. Many geraniums can be grown and flowered under artificial light. Lights are a wonderful aid to the plant breeder who must grow many seedlings to maturity, to the propagator who needs more space to accommodate rooted cuttings, and to the gardener who wants to carry large geraniums safely through the winter. Seedlings grow beautifully and cuttings root rapidly under artificial light. Artificial light can be used to keep old plants green and to bring miniature and dwarf geraniums into flower.

In artificial light culture you must, of course, provide the same good growing conditions you give to plants in natural light: proper growing medium, temperature, water, humidity, ventilation, fertilizer, and pinching or pruning.

Unless you have unlimited space and budget, it is impractical to use artificial light to bring the large zonal geraniums and the big species pelargoniums into bloom. It can be done, all right, but the cost of lamps, power, and space would probably be more than you would care to spend for the results achieved.

The miniature, dwarf, and semidwarf geraniums respond heartily to artificial light culture. Many of the light-loving fancy-leaved geraniums display colors under artificial lights that natural light does not produce.

# KINDS OF ARTIFICIAL LIGHT

Incandescent lamps, the light bulbs we use for reading or working, are often used in greenhouses to force long-day plants into flower, or to break the budding cycle of chrysanthemums and other short-day plants. Plants need a balance of red and blue light rays for good growth. Incandescent lamps emit considerably more red than blue rays, and by themselves are not satisfactory sources of light for plant growth. Much of the energy consumed by an incandescent lamp is converted to heat—heat strong enough to burn leaves if the plants are placed as close to light bulbs as they need to be to derive any benefit from the light. The heat from incandescent lamps can increase the room temperature measurably; most indoor gardeners try to find ways to decrease the temperature in plant rooms, not increase it.

Fluorescent lamps give off very little heat. In relative quantities of the light rays needed by plants, cool white fluorescent lamps are good in both blue and red; daylight lamps are excellent in blue and deficient in red; deluxe warm white lamps are deficient in blue and very good in red; natural lamps are deficient in blue and excellent in red. The various colored fluorescent lamps—green, red, gold, pink, blue, etc.—are unsuitable for horticultural work.

Fluorescent lamps excellent in both blue and red rays, manufactured especially and only for growing plants, are now available. These lamps impart a brilliance of coloring to flowers and foliage which the brightest sunshine cannot equal.

The hobbyist will find, however, that geraniums and other plants grow well under a one-to-one combination of cool white and daylight lamps, or a pair of cool white lamps, or a pair of daylight lamps. Where the heat from incandescent lamps does not create a problem, two 40-watt fluorescent tubes and two 25-watt incandescent bulbs will make a most satisfactory growing unit.

# A BASIC LIGHT SETUP

For a starter unit purchase a pair of 40-watt fluorescent lamps and a reflector to force the light down on the plants. You can make a reflector of plywood painted white or of foil-covered cardboard. Suspend the lights about 18 inches from the growing area.

Light intensity is strongest in the center portion of every fluorescent lamp and weakest at the ends of the lamp.

Fluorescent lamps can be installed in cabinets or bookcases to make garden units. One firm markets a beautiful glassed-in case complete with lights and legs. There are many portable fluorescent setups on the market.

If space permits you can install several pairs of lamps or single strip fixtures. In my study is a lighted plant area underneath built-in bookcases. One daylight and one cool white 96-inch 75-watt lamp make a fine growing unit.

The cost of a pair of 48-inch 40-watt fluorescent lamps, starters, and a reflector is approximately twenty dollars.

I give geraniums 14 to 18 hours of artificial light per day. In our area it costs about one-quarter cent per hour to operate two 40-watt tubes. I use automatic timers to switch the lights on and off, but this can be done manually.

Fluorescent lamps decrease in efficiency as they age. Replace them every six months when used for growing geraniums. You can use the replaced lamps in other areas where strong light is not so vital. Clean tubes give brighter light. Remember to disconnect the lights when cleaning them.

## HOW MUCH LIGHT

Geraniums are true sun lovers but in our windows and greenhouses the intensity of the sun varies, and some days there is no sun. In fluorescent-light gardens the light is constant.

Engineers tell us that intensity of the light decreases in proportion to the distance between lamp and plants. (See Table page 120.) Plants four inches from the tubes receive almost twice as much light as those placed eight inches away. This is a fine arrangement for flat-growing gloxinias and African violets, but most geraniums tend to grow tall and upright. The answer is to place them so leaves nearly touch the lights, and as they grow pinch out the tops to make them bushier.

If gold-leaved geraniums such as 'Damon's Gold Leaf,' 'Golden Oriole,' or 'Verona' show cupped leaves with small indentations, they are not getting enough light. Move them closer to the source of light.

## Table of Illumination in Foot-candles

Illumination of plants at various distances from two or four 40-watt standard cool white fluorescent lamps mounted approximately two inches below a white-painted reflecting surface.

| DISTANCE FROM LAMPS (inches) | ILLUMINATION | | |
| --- | --- | --- | --- |
| | TWO LAMPS* USED** (FC) | FOUR LAMPS* | |
| | | USED** (FC) | NEW (FC) |
| 1 | 1100 | 1600 | 1800 |
| 2 | 860 | 1400 | 1600 |
| 3 | 680 | 1300 | 1400 |
| 4 | 570 | 1100 | 1300 |
| 5 | 500 | 940 | 1150 |
| 6 | 420 | 820 | 1000 |
| 7 | 360 | 720 | 900 |
| 8 | 330 | 660 | 830 |
| 9 | 300 | 600 | 780 |
| 10 | 280 | 560 | 720 |
| 11 | 260 | 510 | 660 |
| 12 | 240 | 480 | 600 |
| 18 | 130 | 320 | 420 |
| 24 | 100 | 190 | 260 |

* Center-to-center distance between the lamps was two inches.
* * These lamps had been used for approximately 200 hours.


# SEEDS AND CUTTINGS

I have started geranium seeds without light, and I have started them directly under artificial lights, and I can discover no difference in germination time. However, once seed has germinated the seedlings grow rapidly under fluorescent lights. I place seedlings at a distance of about four inches from light tube to pot rim. Cuttings root well at this distance, too. If seedlings show top-leaf bleaching or blanching they may be growing at too high a temperature.

Here are some reports on geraniums started from seed and cuttings:

A packet of zonal geranium seed sown in sponge rock in Sep-

97. *Bookcase in author's study is brightened by fluorescent-lighted shelf for dwarf geraniums, and rooted cuttings of other kinds. The unit (hidden by valance) includes two 40-watt fluorescent lamps.* PHOTO BY MEL JACOBSEN

tember showed first germination four days after sowing. Within a week 50 percent had germinated, and germination continued for eight weeks until all but four of the 24 seeds had germinated. Six weeks after sowing six of the seedlings were large enough to transplant easily; with care several others could have been transplanted. The six were planted in thumb pots of soil containing one-third peat moss. Placed four inches from fluorescent lights these seedlings grew rapidly and in another six weeks were ready for transplanting to two and one-half inch pots. Six weeks later they were shifted to three-inch pots. By late April, three months from shifting to three-inch pots and about seven months from sowing, they budded and some of the smaller ones were left to flower under the lights. Others were moved to windowsills. Growers who have struggled twelve months or more getting seedling geraniums to bud at poorly lighted windows find this an unbelievably short time.

Tip cuttings of variegated-leaved 'Wilhelm Langguth' inserted in vermiculite on August 20 were heavily rooted and ready for transplanting on September 7. No earth-shaking record, but it shows that geranium cuttings root as well under artificial light as they do in sunshine.

Robert Waln, Drexel Hill, Pennsylvania, past president of the Men's Garden Clubs of America and an avid artificial-light gardener, has had fine success growing geraniums under lights. He roots cuttings directly into three-inch pots in October, sets them under lights and some of them bloom for the year-end holidays. In January he makes additional cuttings from these plants for his summer garden.

Fluorescent lamps are invaluable for wintering old plants or tree geraniums. Set the plants under the lights, water lightly and let them grow slowly until spring.

If you like to grow miniature or dwarf geraniums, you will find they grow nearly as rapidly under artificial light as in sunshine. It is difficult to give any hard and fast rules regarding placement in relation to the lamps. Place them so leaves are nearly touching the light tubes. They can stand a little more fertilizing under artificial light than in natural light because the constant light makes them grow more rapidly than the off and on sun in a winter window garden.

A friend inserts self-cuttings around her outdoor geraniums in summer. In fall she pots these smaller plants for her indoor winter garden. They initiate buds in midsummer and early fall and continue flowering right through the winter indoors.

Lights are of great help in maintaining compact growth on the fancy little trained trees shown in Chapters 11 and 16.

There is one commandment to obey wherever or however you grow geraniums, including fluorescent-light culture. Do not crowd them! Overcrowding may allow disease to start and it encourages pests.

## FLUORESCENT LIGHTS IN THE GREENHOUSE

Every greenhouse gardener sooner or later faces the fact that his greenhouse space is not large enough to grow all the geraniums he wants. Install fluorescent lights under benches and grow your cuttings, seedlings, and dwarf plants in these spaces.

In an area under the benches in my greenhouse I set potted geraniums directly into sand and gravel, give them steady light from a pair of 75-watt fluorescent lamps, and grow healthy geraniums in space once reserved for low-light plants such as philodendron, cissus, and sansevieria.

A word of caution about using fluorescent or other night lighting in the greenhouse: cover ventilators with screening to keep out the moths attracted by the lights.

Do not put chrysanthemums in garden areas which receive artificial light. They are short-day plants and the lights will delay their flowering.

# 15

## Geraniums in the Greenhouse

There are greenhouses priced to fit every budget: small window greenhouses, plastic houses, lean-to and freestanding greenhouses. It is possible to make a small profit from a home greenhouse. With the popularity of geraniums on the upswing there is a need for more specialists who handle odd and rare geraniums and grow seed for other hobbyists.

My own small greenhouse, 10 feet wide and 12 feet long with a small five-foot workroom, is attached to our house. Since I write about many plants and sell seed of several types, I grow a wide variety of plants in this greenhouse, including geraniums.

In California where geraniums grow outdoors the year round, there are many small greenhouse operators who make a specialty of odd, rare, and hard-to-propagate geraniums. They start seedlings and cuttings in their greenhouses where they can keep an eye on them. One greenhouse owner says she cannot keep up with the demand for unusual, rare, dwarf, scented- and fancy-leaved geraniums.

## GREENHOUSE CULTURE

If you live in an area of long winters, you will really appreciate growing geraniums in a greenhouse, for they do not require the extra heat which many plants must have. Geraniums can be grown to the peak of perfection in night temperatures of 55 to 60 degrees. They withstand temperatures as low as freezing, but when the temperature falls below 50 degrees they stand still and show no new

98. *Geraniums in greenhouse at Merry Gardens, Camden, Maine. Scented-leaved types and miniatures may be seen on the bench and shelf at left, double zonals at right.* PHOTO BY MERRY GARDENS

growth. Geranium leaves may become reddish yellow when grown at temperatures under 50 degrees.

Lady Washington geraniums grow an abundance of leaves when temperatures are over 60 degrees but set flower buds only at temperatures below 60 degrees. If you have not succeeded in getting yours to flower well, reduce the temperature to 60 degrees and within three months you will notice buds appearing on healthy plants.

Almost all geraniums need full sunlight to grow their best. Day length does not affect flowering but light intensity does. Lack of light is one of the reasons many window gardeners fail to get a full quota of flowers from winter-grown geraniums. In greenhouses in

99. *This curved-eave, aluminum-framed home greenhouse fits beautifully into the landscape, and provides for its owner an abundance of sunny bench space for a geranium collection.* PHOTO BY LORD & BURNHAM

which only geraniums are grown it is seldom necessary to apply shading to the glass, although light shading may help reduce summer temperatures.

Do not crowd geraniums. Space them so leaves do not touch. Crowding causes them to grow rangy. In crowded conditions only the topmost leaves get the full benefit of the sun.

Any of the soil mixtures mentioned in Chapter 2 are satisfactory for greenhouse geraniums. A well-drained aerated soil that is moisture retentive and low in fertility makes a splendid geranium soil.

Professional geranium growers check carefully on the calcium and phosphorus content of the soil. Your county agent or state Department of Agriculture can test your soil and tell you if it needs additional amounts of these nutrients. A standard application is about five pounds of ground limestone and five pounds of 20 percent superphosphate per 100 square feet of bench space.

Soil must be pasteurized, for in the greenhouse there is danger of soil-borne pests and disease. Operators of large greenhouses sterilize soil with steam. Home greenhouse owners usually sterilize soil by one of the methods mentioned in Chapter 2.

## WATERING AND FERTILIZING

Hobby gardeners are advised to keep geraniums on the dry side but most greenhouse growers have found that dry soil delays flowering and reduces growth. In the home, where one wages a constant battle against too-high temperatures, it is safer to grow geraniums slowly by keeping them on the dry side. In the greenhouse, under optimum growing conditions, if soil is kept continuously moist (but never saturated) cuttings will root faster and plants will produce a more abundant floral crop.

I like to keep a few of the old pillar-type geraniums in my greenhouse. They make lovely patio decorations during summer and the flowering ones are so pretty in the winter window garden. These tall plants are grown in 10-inch pots. When I first started wintering them in my greenhouse I could not understand why so many of the leaves reddened and dried. Finally, I knocked one of the plants out of its pot and discovered the soil was too dry. A commercial geranium grower mentioned this was a common occurrence especially in spring when greenhouse plants have been grown too dry. Sunny, warm spring days increase transpiration, which in turn increases the plant's need for additional water. Lacking water, the roots and foliage start drying.

Try to moisten geranium soil without wetting the foliage. Wet foliage and flowers invite trouble from disease and pests. Water the surface with a hose or with a watering can. Obviously, seedlings and cuttings growing in small pots cannot use as much water as plants growing in larger pots, and smaller plants require slower watering to keep soil from being dislodged.

Subirrigation saves time. Potted plants are set on gravel in watertight benches and water is applied to the gravel until half the pot is submerged. When topsoil in the pot has become moist, excess water is drained from the bench. This drained water may be conserved in a tank for future waterings.

Automatic constant water level is a watering method favored by many growers. Watertight benches filled with gravel are topped with an inch of sand. Pots are set on the sand and a constant water level is maintained about an inch below the pots. Several growers who use this watering method tell me they have to supplement with surface watering during hot dry summer weather.

Many hobbyists are familiar with the wick watering system. One end of a length of glass wicking is inserted into the bottom or top of the pot and the other end is placed in a pan or trough of water. Greenhouse operators usually line deep trays or troughs with plastic and equip them with a float valve to supply continuous watering through wicks.

For ease of watering consider a type of tube watering, which waters plants individually through plastic tubes. One type, operated manually, waters 32 pots per header and each header can be made to supply various amounts of water to different types of plants or various sized pots. Another type waters 20 pots per tube but all tubes are centrally controlled by a single valve. In addition to watering, either of these systems can be adapted for fertilizing.

Greenhouse growers do not subscribe to the once-a-month fertilizing routine. Modern geranium growers often let their geraniums tell them when they need fertilizer. During sunny warm weather when plants grow fast they demand more fertilizer than in cold cloudy weather.

Soluble fertilizer is preferred to dry fertilizer because it can be distributed more evenly.

As a guide, fertilize twice a month with 20-20-20 or 25-10-10 fertilizer applied at the rate of one-half ounce per gallon of water.


## PROPAGATING

If you are taking only a few cuttings, snap them off as you might snap a string bean. Snapping off terminal cuttings results in rough-surfaced cuttings but diminishes the chance of disease which may be spread through the use of a knife.

When using a blade or knife, dip it in denatured alcohol after each cut. One grower saves old razor blades, sterilizes them, uses one blade per cutting, then discards the blade.

Cuttings taken from soft wood root faster than those taken from hard-stemmed or hardwood geraniums. Cuttings vary in size from one-and-one-half inches for winter cuttings to four inches for summer cuttings.

It is not necessary to let the cuttings wilt before planting them, neither is it necessary to remove most of the lower leaves. Removal of too much foliage takes away the cutting's food supply. However, remove one or two bottom leaves to facilitate inserting the cutting in the rooting medium.

Sand is still the preferred rooting medium although I have obtained excellent results with horticultural grade perlite or vermiculite. If you use sand, water it well the day before you plant your cuttings. Plant the cuttings in flats or pots. Stick them into the sand about one inch and space them an inch apart. Provide mild bottom heat to raise the *soil temperature* to 65 to 75 degrees while maintaining a greenhouse temperature of 55 to 60 degrees. Shade the cuttings for a few days with tobacco- or cheese-cloth. Newspapers used for shading tend to mildew.

Save yourself time and labor by rooting cuttings directly in two-and-one-quarter-inch pots of peat, bagasse, or clay.

Several commercial growers let stock plants grow large and tree-like, then use all the bottom stem cuttings for propagating. One commercial grower lets top branches remain on the plants and sells them as tree geraniums.

*P. domesticum* (Lady Washington geraniums) grown to pillar form produces a marvelous supply of cuttings, and the luxurious foliage head makes an attractive tree form for garden decoration.

When stock is rare I often use an entire plant for propagation, taking first the tip or terminal cuttings, following with single-eye or mallet stem cuttings. Plant the smaller cuttings so the petiole or leaf stem is barely above the rooting medium. (If the node has flowered, discard it as it will not grow a new shoot.) It takes about four months for such cuttings to flower.

## CULTURED CUTTINGS

The grower who gardens for pleasure only will not be too interested in cultured cuttings, but it is advantageous for anyone interested in a profit-making greenhouse to learn something about these cuttings.

With millions of geranium cuttings being sold every year it is understandable that diseases (such as various types of virus) are found in certain strains.

Cultured cuttings, which can be purchased from many sources, are virus-free but they are still subject to other diseases. The process of keeping a record of pathogen-free plants is called culture indexing. It means that thin slices of stem tissue are taken from cuttings and laboratory tested to discover the presence or absence of bacteria.

You can build your own supply of pathogen-free geraniums by growing blocks of plants from cultured cuttings, then testing these plants at regular intervals to see that they are still virus-free.

The operator of a small geranium specialty greenhouse told me he did not start making a real profit until he began growing cultured stock. You may be able to obtain more information on this subject from your state Department of Agriculture. There is a booklet containing excellent information on the subject, titled *Geraniums*. Priced at two dollars, it is available from the publishers through John W. Mastalerz, 207 Tyson Building, Pennsylvania State University, University Park, Pennsylvania.


## GERANIUMS FROM SEED

Many greenhouse operators grow geraniums from seed for pleasure or profit. Seed from species comes true to form but seed from complex hybrids produces a wide variation of plants. Breeders have been working toward seed strains with fixed traits. Currently making news is a geranium strain developed at Pennsylvania State University. Named 'Nittany Lion' (photo 5) for the university's mascot, it is strong, compact, and disease-free. Twelve-inch plants bear large clusters of brilliant red flowers. It is reported to be the first geranium which comes true to color and type from seed, and will give a good crop of salable red geraniums. It takes somewhat longer to grow geraniums from seed than from cuttings, but seed appears to be virus-free.

You may even want to produce your own strain of seed. Pollinating technique is explained in Chapter 4. When working to develop commercial strains it is wise to keep these points in mind: Commercial growers like semidouble geraniums with 10- to 15-petaled flowers, of compact growth. Early maturing plants which will be in good flower for spring sales are most desirable. And it is always wise to work for disease-resistant strains.

The Lady Washington geraniums (*Pelargonium domesticum*) are nearly immune to bacterial stem rot. Breeders at Mr. Bode's Southern California plant station are producing a number of hybrids between the scented-leaved 'Scarlet Unique' and various *P. domesticums.* Mr. and Mrs. Harry May, Long Beach, California, have created a magnificent rose-scented hybrid between 'Scarlet Unique' and *P. domesticum* 'Dawn.'

To develop seed strains with fixed characteristics you will have to inbreed the plants for four or five generations.

Sow seed as described in Chapter 4. In the greenhouse a night temperature of 60 degrees is fine for geranium seedlings. Water only when needed and do not saturate the soil. If seedlings show light cream-colored tips your greenhouse may be too hot. (This often happens when seedlings are grown in the home, especially under fluorescent lights.)

Transplant the seedlings just as soon as you can handle them. You need not wait for true leaves. Start fertilizing seedlings with half-strength soluble fertilizer weekly until they are ready for a second shifting to three- or four-inch pots. Shifted to the larger pots, they can take full-strength fertilizer at weekly intervals from midspring until early fall; biweekly fertilizings from October until spring.

Under optimum conditions it takes about four months from seed to flower.

## PEST AND DISEASE CONTROL

Geraniums in the greenhouse are subject to all the enemies mentioned in Chapter 5. In addition, they may be subject to a few others which seldom attack window- or garden-grown plants.

Good housekeeping practices, which include removal of dead leaves and flowers and spacing plants so leaves do not touch, give you a head start on a healthy geranium program. Weekly spraying with an insecticide such as malathion, lindane, or rotenone prevents invasions of small flies, moths, and aphids. Instant removal of plants infested with insects or infected with disease may prevent an epidemic. Spraying with fungicides staves off many diseases.

Wash your hands thoroughly with hot soapy water after handling ailing plants and disinfect all pots before using them again.

Do not grow geraniums in a hot humid greenhouse. Control the heat and admit fresh air each day.

Edema (dropsy) which sometimes shows on greenhouse geraniums, and occasionally on window-grown plants, can be recognized by water-soaked bumps on backs of leaves and corky spots on stems. This seems to be a systemic condition resulting when plants absorb more moisture than they can give off through transpiration, and usually occurs during cool cloudy weather. Control this disease by giving the plants better ventilation and less water.

Another ailment sometimes associated with cool weather is chlorosis, or yellowing of leaves. Mr. and Mrs. May expressed the opinion that leaf-yellowing on some of the Lady Washington geraniums may be due to a prolonged spell of cool cloudy weather.

The plume moth damages geraniums from coast to coast. This moth rests with wings extended like an airplane, but when in flight its wings resemble plumes. It enters through greenhouse vents and deposits eggs on geranium buds. As the worms emerge they drill through the buds. DDT kills both moths and worms.

## WHICH VARIETIES TO GROW?

If you grow geraniums purely for pleasure, your choice need be limited only by your budget and the size of your greenhouse. If you plan to make a profit from your geraniums, study the market you aim to satisfy, then plan your growing program.

If there are a number of greenhouses and garden stores in your area, the chances of competing successfully for business may be slim. If there are no greenhouses near you, and you want to raise geraniums for spring sales, try some of the popular ones mentioned in Chapter 7. In many areas the Irene varieties, especially the red ones, are the most popular of all. Foliage is lovely and flowers are large and richly colored.

Red is the most popular color for spring sales. Other good commercial reds are low-growing 'Bonfire' and 'Monmouth Red'; weak-stemmed 'Pride of Camden' and 'Better Times'; early-blooming, long-stemmed 'Victory Red' and 'Hildegard' with well-zoned foliage and large red flowers.

In the pink-salmon range consider long-stemmed 'Salmon Ideal' with light salmon-pink flowers; 'Salmon Irene,' lovely large salmon flowers easily shattered; 'Pink Abundance,' heavy-stemmed double reddish-pink flowers; 'Edna,' a pink variation of 'Better Times'; 'California Beauty' with rose-pink white-centered flowers, and its variety Cook's 'Dark California Beauty.'

A few of the good double and semidouble commercial whites are 'Gardenia,' 'White Magic,' 'Snowball,' 'Layton's White,' and 'Madonna.'

There are many other varieties, some of which may suit gardeners in your region. Send for catalogs of geranium specialists and growers who propagate and sell cuttings or seeds and start growing your geraniums for sale.

If you choose to sell rare and odd geraniums, refer to Chapter 13. While it lists just a few of the many unusual geraniums available, you can start making selections from the plants described.

Then there are the deliciously perfumed scented-leaved geraniums to consider. Some of them, such as strawberry-scented, are slow to propagate. Variegated 'Prince Rupert,' a lemon-scented beauty, is so easily overwatered new growers are apt to kill their first ones. (I overwatered the first three I bought.) If you grow them commercially keep a plentiful supply for repeat purchases.

# 16

## Geranium Trees and Other Trained Forms

The gardener who wants to add distinction to his garden will enjoy training and displaying geraniums. They can be grown or fashioned into trees or standards, bonsai, topiary trees, and espaliers. Versatile ivy-leaved geraniums can be used to cover trellises and totem poles.

### GERANIUM STANDARDS OR TREES

In horticulture, a "standard" is a tree, shrub, or herb grown with an erect treelike stem. The finest geranium standards are grown from seedlings or cuttings trained and groomed to perfection.

Select a strong seedling of upright growth. Keep the lower leaves pinched off. When this is done to young geraniums the trunk shows very little scarring. Stake the tree. Secure the trunk to the stake with several plastic ties to keep it growing straight. The support also keeps the slender trunk from being damaged by wind, birds, or people. When the tree has attained the desired height, pinch out the growing tip and the plant will head out and become bushy. It takes about 18 months to develop a geranium tree 36 inches across the top from a seedling, and about 12 months from a strong four- to six-inch cutting.

Any of the strong-growing, upright, scented-leaved geraniums make fine trees. Rose-scented variegated 'Lady Plymouth' and 'Attar of Roses' grow rapidly. 'Snowflake,' with round green-and-white leaves and rosy stems, also rose-scented, makes a lovely tree but is not a rapid grower.

Strong-growing, salmon-flowered zonal geranium 'Mme. Landry' makes a fine standard. Others I have seen grown beautifully include the Painted Lady variety 'Apple Blossom,' single scarlet-flowered zonal 'Inferno,' green-and-ivory fancy-leaved 'Flower of Spring,' and fancy-leaved 'Wilhelm Langguth.'

Two of my own favorites are the novelty geranium 'Mr. Wren' and pink-flowered gold-leaved 'Verona.' Both of these rapid growers are splendid for tree forms.

Water, fertilize, and care for tree geraniums as you would other geraniums. Transplant them when they outgrow their pots. A good height for a geranium tree is 36 inches, but I have seen some fine four-foot trees.

There are some faster ways to grow or make standards. When you are getting plants ready for the spring garden, or when you bring them indoors in fall, select a strong, straight, single-stemmed plant and repot it. Nip off all side growth. Stake it and when it has reached the height you want, pinch out the growing tip and you will have a tree in one season. With care it is possible to root 10- or 12-inch cuttings thus getting a head start on the size of your tree.

Mr. F. G. Read, Norfolk, England, who is famed for his dwarf geraniums, believes that some miniature geraniums can be grown as standards. Varieties which branch freely are not suitable, but ʌ one uses a variety which produces a strong growth with very short nodes, a standard can be produced the second year from cutting or seed. The procedure is the same as outlined above, beginning with the rubbing or nipping off of side growth.

Standards live to a great age. I have friends whose tree geraniums are ten and twelve years of age. Each year they grow more beautiful.

**Wintering Standards.** If you have window space indoors, keep the standards growing as you do your other geraniums. Lacking window space you may be able to store them (for a fee) at a greenhouse. A greenhouse in my area charges a minimum of ten dollars per tree for winter storage. The greenhouse operator told me that some of the same tree geraniums had been stored with him for ten successive winters.

You might find it advisable to winter your tree geraniums under fluorescent lights. Or try one of the other wintering methods described in Chapter 6.

In climates such as Oregon's, where light frost may occur, some

100. *Frankly fake geranium tree made by author of zonal cuttings.*
PHOTO BY MEL JACOBSEN

101. *Author's frankly fake geranium tree starts with wire cone filled with moist sphagnum moss.*
PHOTO BY MEL JACOBSEN

growers winter their geranium trees much as we do rose trees. They dig the tree geranium with all of its attached roots and lower it into a trench. Given a light protection of peat moss mulch and trenched in a protected area, it is ready to be lifted in early spring and started into growth again.

**Frankly Fake Geranium Trees.** Standards add great style to a garden. If you would like one or more for decorative effect, you can make them as easily as you can design a flower arrangement.

To make a three-foot standard, you will need at least six 12-inch geranium cuttings with buds or flowers. Remove two to four of the lower leaves and condition the branches by setting them in room-temperature water in a dark place for a few hours before working with them. These fake trees are effective, too, when made from nonflowering branches or from branches of scented- or colored-leaved geraniums.

Cut a dowel or bamboo cane or strong green garden stake to a

40-inch length. Fill an 8- or 10-inch pot with gravel and small stones. Make a cone-shaped head eight inches across from wire hardware cloth or chicken wire. Slip the cone over the top of the stake, point down, and wire the bottom of the cone to the stake. Fill the cone with moist green sheet moss or Oasis. Insert the conditioned geranium branches in the moist medium, and you will have a ten-minute tree to delight you and impress your guests.

## "CUTTING" OR TOPIARY TREES

It is easy to make a stylish topiary tree from geranium cuttings. Fill a ball of chicken wire with moistened sphagnum moss, fasten it to the top of a potted dowel and cover the ball with geranium cuttings. The colored-leaved geraniums are beautiful used this way, or you can make a neat little topiary from scented-leaved geraniums (photos 65 and 66). For small table trees *Pelargonium crispum* and its small-leaved varieties are most appealing.

Cover the cutting-studded tree head with plastic film and set it away from the direct sun for one or two days before displaying the tree. When cuttings have rooted, transplant them and add new ones to the topiary to maintain its rounded contour.

## PSEUDO BONSAI

Geraniums can be trained to bonsai or artificially dwarfed potted plants. Select a geranium which has become dwarfed through lack of water, fertilizer, or light, or take any small two- or three-inch geranium. Remove from pot and trim the roots halfway back. Repot in a low, squatty bonsai container. When repotting arrange some of the heaviest roots (which are nearest the trunk of the plant) to show above the soil line. Finish by covering the topsoil with pebbles. Any of the dwarf geraniums can be grown in this Oriental fashion. Some of the odd and rare species make splendid bonsai subjects: *Pelargonium* x *divaricatum,* the absinthe geranium, with frilly gray-green foliage is charming in a similarly colored ceramic container; *P. abrotanifolium,* the southernwood geranium, with small divided leaves and red-dotted flowers is ideal for bonsai. All tuberous-rooted geraniums make marvelous bonsai plants.

102. *Pseudo bonsai geranium of* Pelargonium *x* divaricatum. PHOTO BY
MERRY GARDENS

## ESPALIERED GERANIUMS

Espalier means the flat training of plants to fences, trellises, or
garden stakes. Ivy-leaved geraniums are easily trained to espalier
form. Standard geraniums are handsome but more difficult.

Geraniums can be trained to one shoot, a pair of shoots growing
in opposite directions, or in fan-shaped top growth.

Start training the upright kinds when seedlings or cuttings are
about 10 or 12 inches tall. Head back the main stem by nipping
out the growing tip. Then allow the geranium to grow as many
shoots as you believe decorative. As shoots grow, tie them to a

103. *Southernwood-scented geranium* (Pelargonium abrotanifolium) *makes fascinating pseudo bonsai.* PHOTO BY MERRY GARDENS

trellis. Keep side shoots pinched out so there is good spacing between the branches.

The first espaliered geranium I ever grew was the result of an accident. A strong stem of 'Skies of Italy' had been partially broken and bent during the summer. I found its angular growth pleasing and trained a similar growth on the opposite side of a straight central stem. The finished plant resembled a candelabra.

'Sunset,' the gorgeous variegated ivy-leaved geranium, makes a beautiful espalier. Others are dark-red 'Mexican Beauty,' pale-pink 'Comtesse de Gray,' cerise-flowered 'New Dawn,' free-blooming rose-pink 'Sibyl Holmes,' or cerise-purple 'Judy.'

# 17

## Decorating with Geraniums

Hobbyists, decorators, flower arrangers, and landscapers have found varied and imaginative ways to display geraniums indoors and outdoors. Whether you grow one geranium or many, the color and form add a special glow to your various kinds of gardens.

## DISPLAYING GERANIUM COLLECTIONS

There are many good-looking plant stands on today's market that can be used for easy-to-do indoor garden displays.

A friend who prefers pink-flowered geraniums displays low-growing rose-flowered 'Genie,' neon-pink 'Penny,' various pink-flowered bird's-egg and zonal geraniums, and the pink-flowered ivy-leaved trailers 'Alliance' and 'The Blush' on a white wrought-iron plant "tree."

I like a window-garden setup I have close to a south window (photo 3). On a plant table 42 inches long, 18 inches wide, and 14 inches high with a two-inch-deep galvanized steel tray inserted in the top, I alternate flowering, pretty scented-leaved, or colored-leaved geraniums.

A half-inch layer of sponge rock topped with green sheet moss covers the metal tray. The moss and sponge rock are always kept moist to increase the humidity in the air around the plants. Moist green sheet moss plumps up and looks like a carpet of fine grass, making a pretty ground cover for the geraniums. Sometimes this table holds several pots of dwarf geraniums, with ivy-leaved geraniums growing in cholla wood standards or trained as topiary trees

104. *Geraniums make a pleasing appearance in almost any kind of con-*
*tainer. Here they have a special elegance in Italian terra-cotta pots as*
*accents on entryway steps.* PHOTO BY PAUL E. GENEREUX

105. *An old-fashioned window garden drenched by sunlight and filled with a fascinating collection of thriving geraniums. Note wide spacing of plants for ample air circulation.* PHOTO BY PAUL E. GENEREUX

at the corners. (See photos 71 and 73.) A piece of weathered wood picked up in the forest serves as a base for some of the wee geraniums. I sprayed this 20-inch piece of wood a dull gray-green. It is aged just enough to allow the pots to be pushed into the wood, and I can display eight to ten miniature geraniums without crowding. Ivy-leaved geraniums are planted directly into soil-filled hollows in the wood.

When the miniature plants are not in good form, I use the entire tray for displaying other types. Sometimes the garden holds only small pots of scented-leaved geraniums. Slender, upright *P. crispum minor,* 'Scarlet Unique,' and *P. tomentosum* add height to the garden. Ruffled-leaved, red-flowered 'Capri' and 'Mrs. Kingsley' are

106. *Never underestimate what a few geraniums can do around a home garden. Here a half-dozen bright pink zonals transform an entranceway planter into a joyous occasion. Variegated* Vinca major *cascades gracefully over the edge.* PHOTO BY PAUL E. GENEREUX

107. *Geraniums are practically unexcelled for decorating an outdoor living area. These zonals are grouped on a wire rack at the base, and others are held on the wall by special pothangers.* PHOTO BY PAUL E. GENEREUX

added for floral interest. Specimen plants are often displayed singly or in groups of three or four matching or contrasting colors. Occasionally I center a specimen plant of fragrant ruffled-leaved, apple-scented *P. odoratissimum* on a small pedestal or upturned pot and group smaller geraniums around its base.

Near my east kitchen window is a spice shelf holding small plants of geraniums with leaves scented nutmeg, old spice, and ginger.

When I want to create a real conversation piece, I display *P. odoratissimum* with green-and-white-leaved 'Mme. Salleron' (which does not flower) or with the multicolor-leaved 'Skies of Italy,' next to a parrot in a glass dome.

I enjoy growing many other kinds of potted plants, too, and have found sun-loving cacti and succulents, many bromeliads, free-flowering *Begonia semperflorens,* woolly-leaved Begonia 'Fleecealba,' and spring-flowering bulbs to be a few of the many plants which complement geraniums.

A friend has a large south bay-window with a 20-inch-base shelf and two hanging shelves. She specializes in amaryllis, geraniums, and coleus. The combination may sound strange, but her window garden is a blaze of color from early winter until plants go to the summer garden. Taking a cue from her, I made a window planting of rose-margined amaryllis 'Picotee,' and geraniums 'Apple Blossom,' 'Rosebud,' and carnation-petaled, pink-flowered 'Jeanne.' It was so successful I plan to repeat it.

A gardener who dotes on golden-leaved geraniums emphasizes their particular beauty by planting them in handsome glazed pots of bronze, moss-green, or rust-red.

Another who favors colored-leaved geraniums keeps them in trays of pebbles with each pot sitting on a gold-painted brick. The bricks are gilded with a pressurized spray paint, renewed annually.

108. *Author uses piece of weathered wood picked up in forest as a display base for small geraniums.* PHOTO BY MEL JACOBSEN

I have seen hobby collections of geraniums well displayed on hanging glass shelves at doors and windows. One of the loveliest mingled colored-glass bottles with the bright beauty of the geraniums.

A most fetching idea is to plant your window garden generously with colorful geraniums and repeat the color scheme directly outside the window. We have windows which start 14 inches from the floor. The effect when viewed from outdoors or indoors is of one continuous bank of geraniums.

A tea cart makes a fine portable plant table. Mine, used for patio dining in summer, doubles as a plant display table in winter, and occasionally is used to hold seedlings and rooted cuttings. Its mobility allows it to be moved to a lighted window away from the flowering window gardens.

On a garden tour I saw a half-dozen eight-inch pots of watermelon-pink 'Gibson Girl,' a Lady Washington geranium with near-black blotches on its petals, displayed in a stair landing. The use of the one color made the planting appear to be a solid line of color.

Decorative effects can be achieved by adding foliage plants to your flowering geranium collection.

A copper tub or boiler makes a decorative planter for geraniums, blending harmoniously with Early American interiors. Add dark-stained legs as a base for the tub and it fits nicely in modern interiors.

The home of an architect features an indoor window-well made to display plants. Geraniums, azaleas, chrysanthemums, or spring-flowering bulbs take turns being displayed.

At a dinner party I saw a colorful buffet arrangement of red-and-white-flowered geranium 'Double New Life' placed near a tall glass globe filled with polished red apples.

## SCENTED-LEAVED GERANIUMS IN ARRANGEMENTS

Some of my most pleasing "little" arrangements capitalize on the scented-leaved geraniums. Maybe you cannot make, or do not care for, complicated floral arrangements but like easy-to-do arrangements.

Most arrangements can be handled more easily if you work with Oasis, that marvelous material that drinks up several times its weight in water. Get it from a florist or hobby shop. Cut the design you

109. *Author's quick-and-easy informal party arrangement uses red geranium flowers, chrysanthemums, and boxwood in water-saturated Oasis concealed by red papier-mâché container. Red-and-white striped candle adds a holiday touch.* PHOTO BY MEL JACOBSEN

want—block, ball, tree, or spire. Immerse the Oasis in water for a few minutes. Remove, place in container, and start decorating.

It takes only one white flower umbel to make a charming cherry-mint sundae, a clever decoration for a children's party, buffet, or child's room. Cut off all but an inch of the stem and put the flower cluster in the center of the Oasis. Border it with a few leaves of peppermint geranium, top with artificial cherries, and finish with a pair of red-and-white straws. Condition scented geranium leaves by cutting them with their entire stem, immersing to the leaf blade in room-temperature water and letting them stand in the water in a darkened room for four to six hours before using.

To make an attractive candle or peppermint stick, cut a column of Oasis and secure it at intervals with moisture-proof florist's tape.

110. *Author's arrangement of geranium foliage and flowers spilling from a wicker horn of plenty makes a simple but effective decoration. The stems are inserted in water-saturated Oasis concealed inside the container.*
PHOTO BY MEL JACOBSEN

Insert the Oasis column on a pin-type flower holder. Remove the florets from one white and one red geranium cluster. Wire and tape the florets. Stick into the Oasis in alternating or zigzagging rows, one red, one white. Finish the base with peppermint- or rose-scented geranium leaves.

Make an informal party arrangement of geraniums and chrysanthemums based in Oasis and a florist's box of papier-mâché, or in one of your own containers. Center with a gay candle (photo 109).

For a holiday tree, cut Oasis in a cone shape and cover with red geranium flowers. Finish with leaves from one of the pine-scented geraniums: deeply-cut *P. radens* (Crowfoot), ferny *P. denticulatum,* or *P. denticulatum* 'Filicifolium.' You might try an entire tree covered with pine-scented geranium leaves decorated with small ornaments or satin bows.

Geranium bouquets in bean pots are popular favorites. Use geranium flowers only; a combination of scented-leaved, small-flowering species and zonal geraniums; or add other favorite annual or perennial flowers.

Geranium foliage and flowers spilling from a wicker horn of plenty make a simple but effective arrangement.

Arrangers with a gift for designing with unusual flowers will enjoy using *Pelargonium* x *ardens*. Borne on slender stems, the vivid red-and-bronze flowers can turn a commonplace design into a highly interesting one.

The flowers of Lady Washington geraniums make glorious arrangements. Petals on garden-grown plants cling to stems for several days. However, if you use flowers from greenhouse-grown plants, drop a little clear glue into the center of petals to keep them from shattering so quickly.

## LANDSCAPING WITH GERANIUMS

Gardeners are learning how easily geraniums are grown, how little care they require in the outdoor garden, and what an amazing amount of color and variety they provide. With this knowledge, gardeners see boundless opportunities to use geraniums in special plantings.

*111. Geraniums and redwood seem to have a natural affinity for each other. Here a handsome planter provides an ideal spot for growing and showing bright salmon-orange zonals.* PHOTO COURTESY CALIFORNIA REDWOOD ASSOCIATION

Visualize a terraced garden with tiers of solid-colored geraniums —pink, salmon, rose, or red.

A slope or embankment covered with masses of flowering ivy-leaved geraniums is spectacular. Eastern and Midwestern gardeners seldom have enough of these trailers to cover hillsides, but it is possible to use a few plants to advantage as ground cover under a favorite geranium, rose, or fuchsia tree. It is quite easy to have a good display of ivy-leaved geraniums trailing over a retaining wall.

Steps bordered with potted geraniums are colorful from spring to autumn.

If your home has room for no other outdoor adornment, a pair of potted geraniums flanking your entryway will say "Welcome!" to your guests.

Many other ideas for landscaping with geraniums are described in Chapters 1, 2, and 16.

112. *Geraniums are right in step with the space age. Here they form an important part of a contemporary planting design. Black and white marble chips are separated by redwood dividers with brilliant scarlet zonal geraniums for accent.* PHOTO BY LARRY B. NICHOLSON

# 18

## True Geraniums and Related Plants

Few gardeners have more than a nodding acquaintance with the true geraniums, or Cranesbills. Many of these plants have flowers rivaling the beauty of the garden geraniums, or pelargoniums. All have intricately-formed leaves of green, gray-green, or silver. Flowers are in shades of white, pink, red, lavender, and blue. There are single-flowering and double-flowering forms. The Cranesbills or wild geraniums add beauty to rock gardens and paths. Some of the larger kinds are colorful in borders and beds.

There are more than 150 species of true geraniums—annuals, perennials, and biennials—endemic to the temperate zones of the northern hemisphere.

Since many true geraniums have such fine foliage and flowers and are hardy, it would seem a good idea to do some hybridizing among them. I have seen but one such cross, that made by Mrs. Clara May. If it is a sample of possible hybrids, I predict other breeders will want to set to work on similar hybridizing projects. Gardening encyclopedias list a few hybrid forms and often mention the fact that various species interbreed when planted close together.

Several American and European catalogs list a wide variety of true geranium seed and a few specialists list plants. At least one dealer has a listing of thirteen of the choicest species.

Many California *Geraniaceae* enthusiasts grow true geraniums as companion plants for their garden and show geraniums. I saw lovely plantings of *Geranium incisum* with its finely cut leaves and flowers as blue-purple as those of a campanula. Admiring a bed of *G. pratense* (the meadow Cranesbill), with its blue flowers and deeply toothed leaves, I was given some seed and told, "Plant it where you want it to grow for it will not tolerate transplanting."

Native to Wisconsin woods and hills, and found also in many other areas of North America, is *G. maculatum* of lavender-pink flowers. In California I saw a mature plant which had this geranium as one of its parents. The other parent was *G. Robertianum.* The hybrid was a handsome plant. Its bright ferny green foliage with red stems grew in a mound and it was covered with tiny pale pink flowers.

Although most true geraniums grow easily from seed, you may want to consider first those which are obtainable as plants.

*G. Endressii* hails from the Pyrénées and is "nearly evergreen." Its flowers are rose with darker veining and the bottom petals are fringed. *G. grandiflorum* grows to 16 inches. Its large flowers clustered at the top of the peduncle are blue with red veins and a red-purple eye. Its variety, *G. grandiflorum* var. *alpinum,* is a dwarf form but has larger flowers. *G. ibericum* displays open panicles of violet-blue flowers above woolly heart-shaped leaves. A clump is beautiful in bloom and in fall its leaves turn to autumn colors.

*G. macrorrhizum* has richly scented smooth leaves, and flowers of rose, red, or purple. *G. maculatum* var. *album* is the rare white form of *G. maculatum. G. Renardii,* discovered in 1935, has round velvety dark olive-green leaves and violet-centered white flowers. Foliage and flowers are at their best when grown in meager rock garden soil. *G. Robertianum* ('Herb Robert' or 'Red Robin') is a six- to nine-inch annual or biennial with roundish lobed leaves and small crimson flowers. There is a white form, *G. Robertianum* var. *album,* which may have either green or red stems. In California I saw *G. Robertianum* grown to mounds of perfection in moist shady spots.

*G. sanguineum* has one-and-one-half-inch wide crimson flowers with notched petals. Its dwarf forms, white-and-pink *G. sanguineum* var. *album* and *G. sanguineum* var. *lancastriense* are among the loveliest of the dwarf geraniums. Var. *album* sends its long-stemmed white flowers high above the soft green foliage. Var. *lancastriense* is of easy temperament, a marvelous geranium for a beginner. It grows in any good garden soil in any sunny area but, like *G. pratense,* cannot be transplanted once it has attained any sizable growth, so plant it where you want it to grow and do not disturb it.

*G. Wallichianum* shows large purple flowers on decumbent stems. A cultivated form, 'Buxton's Blue,' has violet-blue flowers with white eyes. The species and the variety should be grown in a sheltered

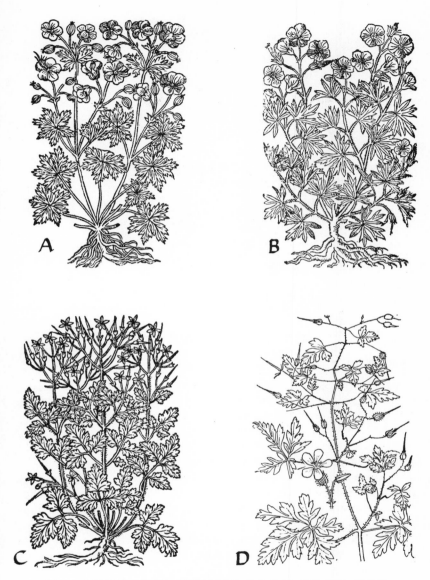

113. *TRUE GERANIUMS FROM SOME OLD HERBALS*

(*A*) *Meadow Cranesbill* (Geranium pratense)
(*B*) *Bloody Cranesbill* (Geranium sanguineum)
(*C*) and (*D*): Variations in *Herb Robert* (Geranium Robertianum)

114. *TRUE GERANIUM FROM AN OLD HERBAL*

*Dove's-foot Cranesbill* (Geranium molle), *described as having mauve, notched petals in flowers a half inch across on plants six to eighteen inches across; native of dry pastures.*

place. *G. dalmaticum*'s bright green foliage turns red in autumn. Its large open flowers are satin pink. *G. stapfianum* var. *roseum,* with glossy cut leaves which take on autumn color, has deep rose cup-shaped flowers on six-inch stems. This rare variety makes a marvelous rock garden plant.

While not all the geraniums are reliably hardy, most of them send out a colony of seedlings each spring. The initial price of the geraniums is not exorbitant.

## GROW THESE FROM SEED

If you like to grow plants from seed you will find many interesting species listed. There is large-leaved, purple-red flowered *Geranium anemonifolium* which needs winter protection in gardens except in frost-free areas. Miniature three-inch-high *G. argenteum* with rosettes of silken leaves and red-veined pink flowers is ideal for rock or handkerchief gardens. Frosty wedge-shaped leaves of *G. cinereum* (or *G. subcaulescens*) enhance its lavender-pink flowers. There are varieties of this one in white, deep rose, crimson, and bright carmine.

Tuberous-rooted *G. Pylzowianum* is a charming diminutive with finely divided green leaves. It is truly hardy but should be planted in good garden soil in a sunny area. Don't be disappointed if you do not see it among the first of your perennials. It is a late spring riser. Mark its growing area, because it is a real treasure.

115. *True* Geranium cinereum (*or* G. subcaulescens) *is a low-growing hardy perennial from the Pyrénées. It has one-inch bright rose flowers.*
PHOTO BY MERRY GARDENS

Twenty-four-inch blue-purple flowered *G. sylvaticum* has a creeping rootstock. There are several varieties of it in white and various shades of rose. Reported to be the finest of all is *Geranium napuligerum*. In her book *Adventures in a Suburban Garden*—which I recommend to anyone interested in true geraniums—Louise Beebe Wilder writes that this choice plant is a very high alpine, that it thrives in an area protected from noonday sun, and that it has large, flat shell-pink flowers which appear nearly all summer long. (The book, published by The Macmillan Company, New York, is out of print; dealers in rare and used books sometimes list it, or your library may have it.)

True geraniums may be propagated from cuttings, divisions, and seed.

## ENCHANTING ERODIUMS

Gardeners partial to miniature plants will surely want to add some *Erodiums,* geranium relatives, to their collections. I became enamored of dainty *E. chamaedryoides* in California and the love affair has extended to other erodiums which I am growing from seed.

Erodium (Heronsbill) is so called from the resemblance of the seed carpels to the head and beak of a heron. It is a genus of about fifty species native to Europe, temperate Asia, and Australia, and sometimes though rarely to South Africa. These intriguing plants have five fertile stamens and five staminodes. Seed is like geraniums or pelargoniums but the tails of the seed twist spirally and the awn or head is hygroscopic or sensitive to moisture. As seed ripens it falls to the ground. When the air is damp, tails untwist, lengthen, and thrust the seed into the soil. If dry weather immediately follows the damp air, these natural hygrometers tighten and pull the seed from the soil to await a more propitious planting time.

Should you desire to grow a few species of these enchanting plants you can have the fun of watching the seeds perform. American dealers list seed of one species, *E. chamaedryoides,* but European sources list several species.

*E. chamaedryoides* is reported to be reliably hardy in Philadelphia and south, but needs special winter treatment in cold areas. This diminutive charmer with its inch-high mat of tiny tufted cordate leaves and its miniature white and pink flowers on half-inch peduncles, is a treasure for a long low container, as a ground covering, or to brighten a sunny bank. In my garden a two-inch pot of *E. chamaedryoides* planted near a bed of rosette-formed sempervivums spread six inches. Divided and repotted in the fall, it wintered in my small greenhouse. It could also be wintered in a cold frame or on a cool sun porch. Several dealers list it, and seeds are in good supply.

True geraniums and erodiums are look-alikes in many ways, but erodiums have every other stamen topped with an anther while geraniums have all ten stamens crested with anthers. Erodiums need to be grown in warm, light, sheltered areas, and they must have good drainage.

## ERODIUMS FROM SEED

Sow erodium seed just as you would pelargonium or geranium seed. Transplant seedlings singly to two-inch pots or put two or three in an azalea pot. Cuttings can be taken in July and rooted in sand, or roots can be divided in early spring or autumn.

At least thirteen species and five varieties of seed can be obtained from American and European dealers.

*E. absinthioides* has thick rootstalks and loose heads of lavender, pink, or white flowers, and hairy tufted leaves. Its variety *amanum* has snow-white flowers and frosty foliage. *E. chrysanthum* bears sulfur-yellow flowers; male and female flowers are borne on separate plants. *E. corsicum* flowers are rosy pink with deep-rose veins and foliage is downy silver. *E. macradenum,* violet flowers with purple spots at the base of two petals, has hairy intricately-cut scented foliage. Its variety, *roseum,* has rose flowers. Purple, violet, or rose "twin" flowers borne on rather weak stems are characteristic of *E. petraeum.*

Annual or biennial *E. gruinum* has two kinds of leaves; lower leaves are undivided, upper three- to five-lobed leaves are heart-shaped. Large violet flowers with deep-colored centers are followed by unique three- to four-inch beaklike seedpods.

Tall 10- to 24-inch *E. Manescavii* has two-inch reddish-purple flowers dotted darker on the two upper petals. Silver-leaved *E. supracanum,* one of the most beautiful of the species, is stemless with two-inch leaves. Its round white petals are veined red.

116. *ERODIUMS FROM AN OLD HERBAL*

*(Left) Hemlock Heronsbill* (Erodium cicutarium) *described as having half-inch pink flowers June to September on a nine-inch plant. (Right) Musk Heronsbill* (Erodium moschatum) *is described as having quarter-inch pink flowers from June to July on six-inch plants. Both are shown in fruit.*

Silken tufted leaves and rose flowers are found on *E. Guicciardii*. *E. Kolbianum,* a hybrid between *E. macradenum* and *E. supracanum,* has white or shell-pink flowers with light veins.

## ANOTHER RELATIVE

Monsonia is a hard-to-find relative of geraniums, but such a statement seldom discourages a true collector. African dealers have sometimes listed seed of this one. I have seen only one plant, at the Mays' in California. Mrs. May said she had waited five years to obtain seed for this apricot-flowered species, which may be *M. speciosa.* Foliage was ferny green. Its cosmos-like flowers close at night. If the plant is moved from filtered sunlight to full sun anytime during the day, the blossoms immediately close. Part of its seedpod is coiled like a spring.

While Monsonia is reported to have about twenty species, only two are mentioned in gardening encyclopedias: *speciosa* and *lobata*. The latter is described as being about a foot high with hairy cordate leaves, and flowers variegated purple, red, white, and green outside, and pale blue with a darker blue inside the petals.

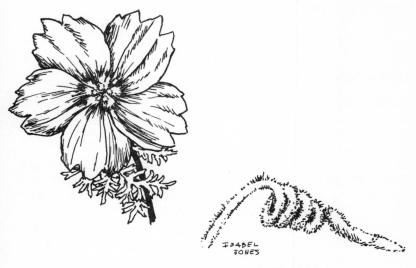

## 117. *THE RARE MONSONIA*

*Artist Isabel Jones drew this botanical detail of monsonia from a 35-millimeter slide taken in the California garden of Clara and Harry May. The cosmos-like, apricot flowers close at night; part of the seedpod is coiled like a spring. This may be* Monsonia speciosa.

# 19

*Geranium Societies, Shows, Projects, and Programs*

## GERANIUM SOCIETIES

*Geraniums Around the World* is the friendly and fascinating publication of the International Geranium Society. In this well-illustrated magazine are articles on culture, new varieties, old ones rediscovered, seasonal pointers on getting the most from your geraniums, and sources of seed and plants. Society membership is four dollars a year, including the magazine. To join this fine group send your check or money order to Mrs. Vernon Ireland, Membership Secretary, 1413 Bluff Drive, Santa Barbara, California. The society has grown from a few dozen members to hundreds, in all states and in many countries, with branches or geranium clubs throughout the United States. If you would like to start a club in your area, Mrs. Ireland will tell you how to go about it.

Geranium societies in Australia and England have large memberships. Many of these geranium enthusiasts also belong to our own society and share their news with readers of *Geraniums Around the World*.

## GERANIUM SHOWS

To show your plants to best advantage, learn some of the grooming tricks practiced by people who win ribbons and trophies for their specimen plants.

Your geranium need not be rare or unusual to be a winner. Show classifications are based on the best specimens.

John C. Tappeiner, Santa Barbara, California, an exhibitor and past show chairman of his local group, suggests these varieties as good ones to groom for showing: Lady Washington varieties 'White Swan,' 'Chicago Market,' 'Dawn,' 'Grand Slam,' 'Orange Sal,' and 'Fifth Avenue'; zonal geranium varieties 'Improved Ricard,' 'Marguerite de Layre,' 'Picardy,' 'White Magic,' 'Better Times,' and 'Salmon Supreme.'

Plan your strategy at least a year ahead of show time, and start new cuttings or shaping established plants nine months before show time. Select cuttings from plants you know to be good growers and heavy bloomers. Plant the cuttings directly into three-inch pots of sand, peat moss, and garden loam. Add a level teaspoonful of bone meal per pot. Spray plants weekly with an aerosol houseplant bomb. Don't wait until pests attack and then try to return the plant to perfection.

Never let your plants show starved yellowed foliage. Fertilize them when the weather is warm and they are growing rapidly. Go easy on fertilizer during cold, cloudy weather. When the plants have reached the final potting stage and show good growth, fertilize them every ten days with any good water-soluble houseplant fertilizer.

Do not allow your plants to dry out completely. When you do water your geraniums, give them a thorough watering. I usually water mine twice just to be on the safe side. Do not water again until the topsoil feels dry or until the pot rings when hit with a piece of metal.

Label the plants correctly—most shows deduct points for incorrect labeling.

Window-grown plants should be turned often to keep them shapely.

Check these details before packing your plants for the show. Have you removed all faded flowers, leaves, and dried stipules? Is the top of the soil clean? If not, scrape it lightly with a knife or small garden implement. Are the pots clean? Scour fertilizer salts and algae from pots; if they will not come clean, coat them with a pot "makeup," a quick-drying, dull-finish paint. Straighten and support plants with stakes. In some geranium shows it is permissible to wire a branch to cover a bare area. Cover up your wiring job with peat moss or pebbles.

Transport plants in large pasteboard boxes. Cut holes in the bottom of the boxes just large enough to fit under the pot rims. Space the holes so leaves from neighboring plants will not touch one another. Use crumpled newspaper as a buffer between pots. Water your plants the night before the show.

## GERANIUM PROJECTS AND PROGRAMS

As garden club editor for *Flower and Garden Magazine* I receive thousands of letters every year from garden clubbers asking for suggested projects, programs, and show themes. Many clubs select one type of flower, shrub, or tree and include something about it in each of their monthly programs. If your club has not explored the exciting subject of *Geraniaceae,* why not make it the theme for next year's study programs?

**Civic Projects.** All over the United States garden clubs and fraternal organizations have launched drives to beautify cities through plantings of flowers, shrubs, or trees. Citizens are asked to dress up their business places or dwellings with planter boxes. As an inducement, the sponsoring organization usually provides the plants at a wholesale price.

In Missoula, Montana, the Moose Drum Corps spends many hours creating and planting flower boxes which are sold to business firms. At season's end merchants may return the boxes and for a small fee the boxes are filled with fresh soil and flowers for the next season. Yucca was used as a central point of interest and ivy added for trailing beauty. Geraniums and petunias are chosen for color and for ease of maintenance.

In Bemidji, Minnesota, the Men's Garden Club beautified streetlight posts with pots of geraniums, petunias, and lobelias. Pot brackets were made at the high school by members of the shop class. Store owners take care of the plants, removing spent blossoms and watering when needed.

The Women's Beautification Committee of Fostoria, Ohio, prettied up their city with pedestal-type planters on parking meters. Geraniums are the highlight of these in the summer; evergreens in winter. Camp Fire Girls, Girl Scouts, and Boy Scouts do the planting. Florists contribute the plants; fertilizer and soil are donated by local business firms.

Four hundred and sixty red and white geraniums were planted at the Wapakoneta, Ohio, High School by members of the Men's Garden Club. This banner of beauty presented a united front with one exception: somehow, four pink geraniums got into the act.

Many garden clubs have made a project of fragrance gardens for the blind. These gardens are filled with aromatic plants and flowers selected not only for scent but for foliage texture. Here the scented-leaved geraniums are at their best. How exciting it must be to see by touching the firm ruffled leaves of *P. crispum,* the beautifully cut leaves of fragrant *P. graveolens,* or the feltlike mint-scented leaves of *P. tomentosum.*

The members of some garden clubs take small tray favors to homes for the aged. A few scented geranium leaves add immeasurably to the appeal of these small bouquets.

If your club handles arrangements for the public library, consider adding a few sprays of scented geranium foliage.

Successful money-raisers at bazaars are sachets or jars of potpourri made from scented geranium leaves. Small plants of scented- or colored-leaved geraniums sell on touch or sight when displayed at the bazaar's plant counter.

**Geranium Programs.** "We've given every type program we can think of. Please help us dream up some new ones." This plaint comes to me dozens of times weekly.

In going through hundreds of yearbooks designed by garden clubs, I find few different geranium projects or programs. Yet geraniums are widely grown. They are frequently mentioned for planting window boxes; for use as bedding plants; or in a program devoted to easy-to-care-for houseplants. Perhaps the following projects and program suggestions will give you inspiration.

Choose geraniums as your flower of the year. Ask members to make scrapbooks of pictures and articles on culture of geraniums and bring them to be judged at a stated time.

Have a summer workshop, using geraniums with annuals and foliage for arrangements.

Dry or press true geraniums for plaques or pictures. (Garden geraniums do not dry well but true geraniums dry beautifully.) Dry them face up, two weeks in the sand. The foliage of some garden geraniums dries very well. Fancy-leaved foliage, as that of 'Skies of Italy,' dries ten days in sand, borax, or silica gel, has beautiful coloring, and makes an unusual addition to a dried arrangement.

Have an arrangement program showing easy ways to create geranium and companion-plant arrangements. Example: a wicker horn of plenty; moistened Oasis in foil is placed in the horn, flowers and foliage are strewn out from the Oasis. Example: Colonials, cone-shaped flower-filled holders to be carried in the hand are charming when centered with geraniums and outlined with pink or blue cornflowers.

Use as a program topic, "Dwarf and Miniature Geraniums—Pretty Space Savers."

Ask a local florist, or perhaps a local member of the International Geranium Society, to present a program on "Knowing, Growing, and Showing Geraniums."

Two geranium programs which have appeal are "Winter Beauty with Geraniums," and for those who do not window-garden, "How to Winter Your Geraniums."

"Ivy-leaved Geraniums, Plants of Multiple Merit" is a good spring-program topic, for these plants are so valuable for boxes and baskets.

"Geraniums in Container Gardens" is also a good subject for a spring or summer program.

Propagating, pruning, or growing geraniums from seed make excellent program topics. Perhaps some member would donate bee-pollinated seed for a junior program. An experienced grower could show the youngsters how to husk the seed. They would have a delightful time learning the knack of seed husking, for these smooth little seeds have a tendency to jump out of their split husks.

"Training and Caring for a Geranium Tree" makes a fine program any time. (See Chapter 16.)

When you plan a program on bonsai, include geraniums. In programs on espaliers, tell how to espalier a geranium.

If there is a geranium specialist in your vicinity, perhaps you can obtain permission for your entire group to visit the nursery. The Wilson Brothers, Roachdale, Indiana, geranium specialists, entertain many garden groups every year. Appointments must be made months in advance but your group will be thrilled with the thousands of geraniums.

**Show Themes.** With new geranium clubs being established all over the country, it is only natural that members want to hold shows to display their hobby plants. Aside from planning the show, one of the big details is deciding on a show theme. Here are several titles to help you on your way:

"Geraniums—Garden Jewels," "Geranium Galaxy," "Summer Fantasy," "A Festival of the Arts," "Geraniums Around the World," "The Sound of Music," "Dramatic Beauty," "A Showcase of Beauty," "Parade of Months," "Language of Geraniums," "Living with Geraniums Through the Year," and "Signs of Summer."

# 20

*How and Where to Buy Seeds and Plants of Geraniums and Pelargoniums*

## SHIPPING GERANIUMS

Before shipping geraniums out of your state, check with your state Department of Agriculture for regulations governing shipments to other states. No permit is needed for mailing seed.

If you are shipping cuttings which will be in transit only two or three days, insert the cuttings in plastic bags, fasten the end of the bag, and the cuttings should arrive safely. If they will be in shipment more than a few days, better insert them in moistened sphagnum moss before placing them in the plastic bag.

Geranium plants are shipped in peat moss, bagasse, or plastic pots. Clay pots are too heavy for shipping. When shipping small or miniature plants place a wad of moistened sphagnum moss on the topsoil, slip a piece of masking tape over each side of the soil and moss, and fasten it to the side of the pot. Cover the plant with a plastic bag, stick the plant label through the bag and into the soil. Fasten the bag with a rubber band or plastic tie. Roll the bagged plant in newspaper. Line the bottom of the shipping carton with several thicknesses of newspaper. Insert the bagged and wrapped plants and they are ready for a safe journey.

If you want to buy geraniums or other plants from outside the United States, you must obtain an import permit. Supply the following information: type of plants to be shipped into the United States, name and address of the shipper, and your name and address. Send the information to United States Department of Agriculture, Bureau of Plant Quarantine, 209 River Street, Hoboken, New Jersey.

## SOURCES

For speedy service, enclose a stamped, self-addressed envelope with your request for a list or catalog.

Arndt Nursery, Hightstown, N.J. All types. No catalog.

Avalon Geranium Gardens, Compton, Calif. Zonal, ivy-leaved, regal. Illustrated list. Wholesale.

Bachman's, 6010 Lyndale Ave. S., Minneapolis, Minn. Zonal, ivy-leaved, some scented-leaved, trees. No catalog.

Barrington Greenhouses, Old White Horse Pike, Atco, N.J. Dwarf, scented-leaved, colored-leaved, some zonal. Catalog 25¢.

Bode's Southern California Geranium Gardens, R. 4, Box 403, Escondido, Calif. Extensive listing, all types. Catalog, *wholesale only*.

W. Atlee Burpee Co., Philadelphia, Pa. Geranium seed. Catalog.

Cook's Geranium Nursery, 712 N. Grand, Lyons, Kans. All types, including odd and rare. Catalog.

Correvon Fils, Chêne-Bourg, Geneva, Switzerland. Seed of hardy or true geraniums and erodiums. Catalog.

Edelweiss Gardens, Allentown, Robbinsville Road, Robbinsville, N.J. Dwarf, scented-leaved, and fancy-leaved kinds. Catalog.

F. G. Read Nurseries, Deopham, Wymondham, Norfolk, England. Seed of dwarf geraniums. Wholesale only.

Gerry's Geranium Garden, 11501 East Massinger, Artesia, Calif. Extensive list of many kinds. Catalog.

Geo. W. Park Seed Co., Greenwood, S.C. Many kinds of geranium seeds. Catalog.

Harry E. Saier, Dimondale, Mich. Seed of zonal and true geraniums, and erodiums. Catalog 30¢.

Henley Floral Co., 1510 S. Walnut St., Hartford City, Ind. Lady Washington (*P. domesticum*) only. Catalog. *Wholesale only*.

Hilltop Farm, R. 3, Box 216, Cleveland, Texas. Scented- and fancy-leaved types. Catalog.

Holmes C. Miller, 280 West Portola Ave., Los Altos, Calif. Extensive listing of all types except *P. domesticum*. Catalog.

Logee's Greenhouses, 55 North St., Danielson, Conn. Scented-leaved, fancy-leaved, ivy-leaved, dwarf, odd and rare types. Catalog 25¢.

Manhattan Garden Supply, 304 N. Sepulveda Blvd., Manhattan Beach, Calif. Extensive listing of all types, including collectors' items and some erodiums. Catalog.

Merry Gardens, Camden, Maine. Extensive listing of all types, including species, odd and rare sorts and collectors' items. Catalog 25¢.

Mr. and Mrs. Harry May, 2258 Roswell Ave., Long Beach 15, Calif. Pelargonium hybridizers; proven varieties introduced through Bode's Southern California Geranium Gardens, which see.

Pearce Seed Co., Moorestown, N.J. Seed of zonal and true geraniums. Catalog.

Schmidt Nursery, 355 Lambert Ave., Palo Alto, Calif. All types. No shipping, no catalog.

Southern California Geranium Gardens. See Bode's Southern California Geranium Gardens.

Stonecrop Nurseries, Inc., Cold Spring, Putnam County, New York. Extensive listing of true geraniums. Catalog.

Temple's Pelargonium Farm, R. 1, Box 113, Fallbrook, Calif. Listing of numerous types of seed.

Thompson & Morgan, Ipswich, England. Seed of zonal and some scented-leaved, true geraniums, and erodium. Catalog 25¢ U.S. funds.

Tonkadale Greenhouses, 3739 Tonkawood Road, Hopkins, Minn. Zonal, some dwarf, scented-leaved, trees. No catalog, no shipping.

Vi's Select Seed Shop, 307 S. Maple, Watertown, S. Dak. Seed kits. No catalog.

Village Hill Nursery, Williamsburg, Mass. Limited list of scented-leaved geraniums. Catalog.

Wilson Bros., Roachdale, Ind. All types of geranium plants. Several kinds of seed. Catalog.

# Index

Absinthe geranium (*P.* x *divaricatum*), 110, 137, 138
'Advance,' 53
*Adventures in a Suburban Garden* (Wilder), 156
'African Belle,' 95
Air layering, 27
'Alice de la Vergne,' 54
'Alliance,' 93, 140
'Alpha,' 9, 65, 66, 70
'Amour,' 97
'Ann Sothern,' 54
Aphids, 41
'Apple,' 73, 74, 77, 78
'Apple Blossom,' 51, 104, 105, 135, 145
'Apricot,' 77
'Apricot Queen,' 93
Arndt, Milton, 56
Artificial light, 117–23
  basic setup for, 118–19
  in greenhouses, 122–23
  kinds of, 118
  for seeds and cuttings, 120–22
'Attar of Roses,' 75, 134
'Attraction,' 65
'Aureum marginatum,' 93
Ayton, Anthony C., 43
'Aztec,' 94

Bacterial leaf spot, 39
Behringer, Clarence F., 52
Behringer, Irene, 52
'Berkeley Belle,' 54
'Better Times,' 48, 132
'Bimbo,' 95
Bird's-egg geraniums, 106–7
'Black Jubilee,' 70
'Black Lace,' 9, 95

Blackleg (cutting rot), 41
'Black Magic,' 97
Black Magic (commercial mixture), 11
Black rot. *See* Stem rot
'Black Top,' 99
'Black Vesuvius,' 56
*Blandfordianum* (*P. denticulatum*), 77
Bloody Cranesbill (*G. sanguineum*), 152, 153
Blossom-blight, 40
'Blossomtime,' 54
'Blush, The,' 140
Bode, Fred A., Jr., 30, 33, 38, 54–55, 70, 99, 131
'Bonfire,' 132
Bonsai, use of geraniums in, 6, 82, 110, 137, 138, 139
Both, Ted, 72
Botrytis leaf spot, 40–41
'Brilliant,' 79
'Bronze Beauty,' 68, 70
Bruant zonal (French-type) geraniums, 54. *See also specific varieties*
Butterfly geraniums, 71
'Buxton's Blue,' 152

Cactus-flowered geraniums, 104–6
'California Beauty,' 133
'Capri,' 142
'Caprice,' 99
'Carefree,' 99
'Carlos Uhden,' 91, 93
'Carmel,' 53, 108
Carnation-flowered geraniums, 106
Case, David, 56
Caterpillars, 42

'Cerise Carnation,' 106
Chandler, Philip A., 37
'Charles Monselet,' 93
'Charles Turner,' 48, 89, 93
'Cheerio,' 54
'Chicago Market,' 96
Chlorosis, 132
'Chorus Girl,' 96
Civic projects, 162–63
'Clorinda,' 73, 79
'Cloth of Gold,' 68
Colchicine, 30
'Comtesse de Gray,' 139
'Concolor Lace,' 79
'Confetti,' 94, 97
Containers, 17–19
    potting, 20–22
'Cook's Scarlet & White Rosebud,' 104
Cranesbill. *See* True geraniums
'Crispum Minor,' 81
'Crocodile,' 93
'Crowfoot,' 77, 148
'Crystal Palace Gem,' 65, 71
Cultured cuttings, 129–30
Curly top, 41
Cutting rot (blackleg), 41
Cuttings, 24, 25–27
    artificial light and, 120–22
    cultured, 129–30
    of fancy-leaved geraniums, 72
    in greenhouses, 128–30
    of ivy-leaved geraniums, 87–88
    of scented-leaved geraniums, 82
Cycocel, 29

'Dahlia Flowered,' 108
'Damon's Gold Leaf,' 119
'Dancer,' 60
'Dark Beauty,' 9, 71
'Dark California Beauty,' 133
'Dark Venus,' 97–99
'Dawn,' 48, 131
'Debonair,' 54
Decorating, 140–50
    displaying collections, 140–46
    landscaping, 149–50
    scented-leaved arrangements, 146–49
    *See also specific varieties*
Dillenius, Johann Jakob, 3
Diseases, 37–41
    control in greenhouses of, 131–32

"Diseases of Geraniums in California" (bulletin), 37
'Distinction,' 71
'Doc,' 58
Double-flowering geraniums, 47–52, 54–55
    *See also specific varieties*
'Double Lavender Pink,' 106
'Double Lilac White,' 91, 93
'Double New Life,' 146
Dove's-foot Cranesbill (*G. molle*), 154
'Dr. Livingston,' 75
Dropsy (edema), 132
'Dubonnet,' 96
Dwarf geraniums, 56–64
    artificial light and, 122
    displaying of, 58
    fancy-leaved, 71
    list of, 63
    as standards, 135
    *See also specific varieties*

Edema (dropsy), 132
'Edna,' 133
Eelworms, 42
'E. H. Trego,' 93
'Elégante, L'' ('Sunset'), 87, 88, 89, 91, 139
'Emma Hossler,' 59, 60
'Empress of Russia,' 98
Erodium, 2, 156–58
*Erodium absinthioides,* 157
*Erodium chrysanthum,* 157
*Erodium cicutarium,* 158
*Erodium corsicum,* 157
*Erodium gruinum,* 157
*Erodium Guicciardii,* 158
*Erodium Kolbianum,* 158
*Erodium macradenum,* 157, 158
*Erodium Manescavii,* 157
*Erodium moschatum,* 158
*Erodium petraeum,* 157
*Erodium supracanum,* 157, 158
Espaliered geraniums, 138–39

'Fair Ellen,' 75, 78
'Fairy Tales,' 59
Fancy-leaved geraniums, 65–72, 117
    culture of, 68–72
    propagating of, 72
'Fanfare,' 54

Fertilizing, 16–17
  in greenhouses, 128
  of miniatures, 57
  for show plants, 161
'Fiat,' 54
'Fiat Enchantress,' 28
'Fiat Queen,' 49, 54
'Filicifolium,' 77, 148
'Filigree,' 69–70
'Finger Bowl' ('Lemon Crispum'), 81
'Firedancer,' 99
'Flag of Denmark,' 107
'Fleurette,' 59, 60
*Floricultural Cabinet and Florist Magazine,* 33
*Florists' Review* (publication), 37–38
'Flower Basket,' 9
'Flower of Spring,' 135
Fluorescent lamps. *See* Artificial light
'Forty-niner,' 65
'Fraîcheur,' 108
'Freak of Nature,' 65
French-type (Bruant zonal) geraniums, 54. *See also specific varieties*

'Galilee,' 89, 93
'Gardenia,' 133
'General Leonard Wood,' 54
'Genie,' 48, 140
*Geraniaceae,* 2
*Geraniaceae* (Sweet), 4
*Geraniologia de Brutelle* (L'Héritier), 4
*Geranium,* meaning of word, 2
*Geranium anemonifolium,* 154–55
*Geranium argenteum,* 155
*Geranium cinereum* (*G. subcaulescens*), 155
*Geranium dalmaticum,* 154
*Geranium Endressii,* 152
"Geranium Grafting" (paper), 28
*Geranium grandiflorum,* 152
*Geranium ibericum,* 152
*Geranium incisum,* 151
*Geranium macrorrhizum,* 152
*Geranium maculatum,* 152
*Geranium molle,* 154
*Geranium napuligerum,* 156
*Geranium pratense,* 151–52, 153
*Geranium Pylzowianum,* 155
*Geranium Renardii,* 152
*Geranium Robertianum,* 152, 153

*Geranium sanguineum,* 152, 153
*Geranium stapfianum,* 154
*Geranium subcaulescens* (*G. cinereum*), 155
*Geranium sylvaticum,* 156
*Geranium Wallichianum,* 152
*Geraniums* (booklet), 130
*Geraniums Around the World* (publication), 28, 29, 160
Germination, 34–36
'Giant Oak,' 75
Gibberellic acid, 28–29
'Gibson Girl,' 97, 146
'Gold Rush,' 71
'Golden Oriole,' 70, 119
'Gooseberry,' 81
Grafting, 24, 27–28
'Grand Slam,' 97, 98
'Grape Leaf,' 74, 82, 83
Gray mold, 40
Greenhouses, 124–33
  cultured cuttings and, 129–30
  fluorescent light in, 122–23
  pest and disease control in, 131–32
  propagating in, 128–29
  watering and fertilizing in, 127–28
'Grey Lady Plymouth,' 77
'Grossmama Fischer,' 97
Growing medium. *See* Soil
Growth stimulants and regulators, 28–29

'Halo,' 97
'Happy Thought,' 65, 71
Hartsook, Frances, 71–72, 99
Hemlock heronsbill (*E. cicutarium*), 158
'Herb Robert,' 152, 153
Héritier, L' (botanist), 3
Heronsbill. *See* Erodium
'Hildegard,' 132
Hill, Mrs. Bruce, 56
'Hills of Snow,' 69
'Honeymoon,' 51
Hormone powder, 25
Horseshoe geraniums (*P. frutetorum*), 9, 71–72
'Hula,' 99
'Hulda Conn,' 104
Humidity, 14–16
Hybridizing, 30–36
  naming new cultivars, 33
  from seed to flower, 34–36

'Imp,' 56
Import permits, 165
'Improved Ricard,' 30, 48
Incandescent lamps, 118
'Inferno,' 135
International Geranium Society, 28, 33, 160
'Irene,' 33, 50, 52, 132
'Irma,' 93
Ivy-leaved geraniums (P. peltatum), 39, 87–93
  culture of, 87–89
  displaying of, 89–92
  espaliering of, 138
  varieties of, 93
  See also specific varieties

'Jeanne' ('Sweet William'), 106, 145
Jenkinsonia cranesbill (P. tetragonum), 1, 116
'Joseph Warren,' 89, 91, 93
'Joy Lucille,' 77
'Jubilee,' 65, 67, 70
'Judy,' 139

'Kleiner Liebling' ('Little Darling'), 56, 60, 61
Knotted storksbill (P. gibbosum), 111, 112

'Lady Cullum,' 65, 69
'Lady Dryden,' 54
'Lady Mary,' 81
'Lady Plymouth,' 75, 134
'Lady Pollock,' 28
Lady Washington pelargoniums (P. domesticum), 1, 22, 28, 39, 94–102, 129, 131, 132, 149
  culture of, 99–102
  temperature and, 125
Landscaping, 149–50
'Lavender Ricard,' 54
'Layton's White,' 133
Leaf curl, 41
Leaf mold, 11
Leaf spots, 40–41
  bacterial, 39
'Lemon Crispum' ('Finger Bowl'), 81
Light, 12–14, 125–26
  for fancy-leaved geraniums, 68
  See also Artificial light
'Lilac White,' 91, 93
'Limoneum,' 81

Lindstrom, R. H., 29
'Little Darling' ('Kleiner Liebling'), 56, 60, 61
'Little Gem,' 75, 76, 78
'Little Read's,' 34
'Little Trot,' 71

McWhorter, Frank P., 37, 39
'Madonna,' 133
'Magenta MacMahon,' 70
'Magenta Rosebud,' 104
'Magenta Ruby,' 52
'Magic Lantern,' 72
'Magnificent,' 48
'Maréchal MacMahon,' 65, 70
'Marguerite de Layre,' 53
'Marie Vogel,' 97
Martha Washington. See Lady Washington pelargonium
'Maxime Kovalevski,' 53
May, Clara, 97, 111, 131, 132, 151, 158
May, Harry, 97, 131, 132
Meadow Cranesbill (G. pratense), 151–52, 153
Mealy bugs, 42
'Medallion,' 70
'Melissa,' 99
'Mexican Beauty,' 89, 90, 93, 139
Miller, Holmes, 56, 69, 70, 104
Miniature geraniums, 56–64
  artificial light and, 122
  displaying of, 58–60
  list of, 63
'Minnetonka,' 24
'Mint-scented Rose,' 75, 76
'Mischief,' 104
'Miss Burdett Coutts,' 67, 69
'Mme. Buchner,' 24, 28
'Mme. Landry,' 134–35
'Mme. Salleron,' 71, 144–45
'Mme. Thibaut,' 106
Moisture requirements, 14–16
  humidity, 14–16
  watering, 14, 19, 127–28
'Monmouth Red,' 132
Monsonia, 158–59
Monsonia lobata, 159
Monsonia speciosa, 158–59
Moore, Harold E., Jr., 74
'More Mischief,' 104
'Morning Star,' 104
'Mosaic,' 72

Mosaic virus, 41
Moss
    peat, 11, 57
    sphagnum, 15, 17, 19, 20, 25, 27
Moths, 42
'Mountain of Snow,' 69
'Mr. Everaarts,' 59
'Mr. Wren,' 24, 108, 135
'Mrs. Cox,' 65, 69
'Mrs. J. J. Knight,' 107
'Mrs. Kingsley,' 79, 142
'Mrs. Layal,' 97, 100
'Mrs. Parker,' 69
'Mrs. Pollock,' 65
'Mrs. Taylor,' 73, 79
Munnecke, Donald E., 37
Musk heronsbill (*E. moschatum*), 158
Mutations, 30
'Mystery,' 99

'Natalie Webster,' 51
Nematodes, 42
'New Dawn,' 90, 139
'New Life,' 107
'Nittany Lion,' 8, 130
'Noel,' 104, 106
Nurseries, list of, 166–67
'Nutmeg,' 77

Oasis (decorating material), 146–48
'Old Spice,' 77
'Orange,' 81
Orange tortrix, 42

'Painted Lady,' 54
'Parisienne,' 97
Pasteurization of soil, 12, 127
'Paul Crampel,' 53
Paulsen, Michael D., 27–28
Paulus, Albert O., 37
Peat moss, 11, 57
*Pelargonium*, 2–3
*Pelargonium abrotanifolium*, 82, 137, 139
*Pelargonium acerifolium*, 109
*Pelargonium acetosum*, 108–9
*Pelargonium angulosum*, 94
*Pelargonium* x *ardens*, 109, 149
*Pelargonium Burtoniae*, 110
*Pelargonium carnosum*, 110
*Pelargonium cordifolium*, 110
*Pelargonium corianderifolium*, 110

*Pelargonium crispum*, 73, 86, 137, 142
    list of, 81
    *See also specific varieties*
*Pelargonium cucullatum*, 94
*Pelargonium dasycaule*, 109, 110
*Pelargonium denticulatum*, 73, 148
    list of, 77
*Pelargonium* x *divaricatum*, 110, 137, 138
*Pelargonium domesticum*, 1, 22, 28, 39, 94–102, 129, 131, 132, 149
    culture of, 99–102
    temperature and, 125
*Pelargonium echinatum*, 110
*Pelargonium ferulaceum*, 110
*Pelargonium formosum*, 110, 111
*Pelargonium fragrans*, 73, 74, 77, 78
*Pelargonium frutetorum*, 9, 71–72
*Pelargonium fulgidum*, 73, 75, 99, 111
    list of, 79
    *See also specific varieties*
*Pelargonium gibbosum*, 111, 112
*Pelargonium glaucifolium*, 111
*Pelargonium graveolens*, 73, 74, 85, 86
    list of, 75
    *See also specific varieties*
*Pelargonium grossularioides*, 82
*Pelargonium hortorum*, 1, 24, 39, 47–55
    fancy-leaved, 65–72
    favorite, 55
    miniature, dwarf, and semidwarf, 56–64
    *See also specific varieties*
*Pelargonium inquinans*, 47
*Pelargonium nervosum*, 82
*Pelargonium odoratissimum*, 33, 73, 144
    list of, 77
*Pelargonium peltatum*, 39, 50, 87–93, 139
    culture of, 87–89
    displaying of, 89–92
    varieties of, 93
    *See also specific varieties*
Pelargonium pomanders, 84
*Pelargonium quercifolium*, 73
    list of, 75
    *See also specific varieties*
*Pelargonium radens*, 74, 77, 148

*Pelargonium ranunculophyllum,* 33, 112
*Pelargonium rapaceum,* 33, 112
*Pelargonium reniforme,* 1, 112–13
*Pelargonium* x *rutaceum,* 113
*Pelargonium salmoneum,* 113, 114
*Pelargonium scabrum,* 113
*Pelargonium scandens,* 114, 115
*Pelargonium Scarboroviae,* 82
*Pelargonium* x *Stapletonii,* 115
*Pelargonium tabulare,* 115–16
*Pelargonium tetragonum,* 1, 116
*Pelargonium tomentosum,* 73, 74, 142
list of, 77
*Pelargonium torento,* 82
*Pelargonium vitifolium,* 74, 82, 83
*Pelargonium zonale,* 47
"Pelargoniums in Cultivation" (Moore), 74
Pennsylvania State University, geranium development at, 130
'Penny,' 140
'Peppermint,' 77
'Peppermint Stick,' 107
Pests, 41–42
control in greenhouses of, 131–32
'Pheasant's Foot,' 77
'Phlox,' 108
'Pigmy,' 56
Pinching, 22–24
'Pink Abundance,' 133
'Pink Alpha' ('Pink Harry Hieover'), 70
'Pink Cloud,' 30, 48, 49
'Pink Conspicuous,' 99
'Pink Happy Thought,' 66, 71
'Pink Harry Hieover,' 70
'Pink MacMahon,' 70
'Pink Poinsettia,' 104
'Pink Rosebud,' 104
'Pistachio,' 65
Plume moth, 132
'Poinsettia,' 104
Poinsettia-flowered geraniums, 104–6
Pollination, 31–33
'Pollock 137,' 67
Pomander balls of scented-leaved geraniums, 84
Potting, 20–22
See also Containers
'Pride of Camden,' 132
'Prince Bismarck,' 71
'Prince of Orange,' 80

'Prince Rupert,' 81
'Prince Rupert Variegated,' 81, 82, 133
'Princess Fiat,' 48, 49
'Princess Victoria,' 50
'Prize,' 54
Programs, 163–64
Projects, 162–63
Propagating, 24–28
air layering, 27
of fancy-leaved geraniums, 72
grafting, 27–28
in greenhouses, 128–29
of scented-leaved geraniums, 82
See also Cuttings; Seeds
Pruning, 22–24
'Puff,' 104
'Pungent Peppermint,' 77

'Rapture,' 97
Rare species pelargoniums, 108–16
Read, F. G., 135
'Red Cloud,' 30
'Red Copper,' 99
'Red-flowered Rose,' 75, 76
'Red Irene,' 52
'Red Robin,' 152
'Red Spider,' 61, 104
Red spiders, 42
Red sweetheart geranium (*P.* x *Stapletonii*), 115
Reflectors, 118
Regals. See Lady Washington pelargoniums
Regulators, growth, 29
'Ricard,' 30, 48
Rober, Ernest, 56
'Rober's Lemon Rose,' 75
'Roderick Dhu,' 71
'Rollinson's Unique,' 79
'Rose,' 75
Rose-scented geraniums. See *Pelargonium graveolens*
'Rosebud,' 145
Rosebud geraniums, 103–4
'Rosy Dawn,' 61
'Royal,' 72
'Royal Fiat,' 30, 48
*Royal Horticultural Society Journal* (publication), 43

'Salmon,' 93
'Salmon Ideal,' 133

'Salmon Irene,' 133
'Salmon Queen,' 53
'Salmon Supreme,' 54
'Santa Paula,' 89, 90, 91, 93
'Scarlet Beauty,' 93
'Scarlet Rosebud,' 104
'Scarlet Unique,' 79, 80, 99, 131, 142
Scented-leaved geraniums, 73–86
  in arrangements, 146–49
  displaying of, 82–85
  groups of, 75–82
  history of, 73–74
  propagation of, 82
Schmidt, William E., 56, 97
Schweitze, Robert, 23
Seeds:
  artificial light and, 120–22
  erodiums from, 157–58
  pollination of, 31–33
  starting plants from, 34–36, 130–31
  true geraniums from, 154–56
  where to buy, 166–67
Semidouble geraniums, 54–55
Semidwarf geraniums, 56–64
  displaying of, 58–60
  list of, 64
Shipping, 165
'Shocking,' 33
Shows, 160–61
  themes for, 164
'Shrubland Rose,' 78, 79
'Sibyl Holmes,' 139
'Silver Stars,' 104
'Single Cerise,' 107
'Single Coral,' 107
Single-flowering geraniums,    53–54.
  See also specific varieties
'Single Light Pink,' 107
'Single New Life,' 107
'Single Rose Pink,' 107
'Skeleton's Unique,' 75
'Skies of Italy,' 65, 66, 69, 139, 145,
  163
'Sneezy,' 62
'Snowball,' 48, 50, 133
'Snowflake,' 74, 75, 77, 134
Societies, 28, 33, 160
Soil, 10–12
  in greenhouses, 126–27
  pasteurization of, 12, 127
Soil detergent, use of, 14, 68, 85, 89
'Southern Cross,' 104

Southernwood geranium (P. abrotani-
  folium), 82, 137, 139
'Sparkle,' 48
Species Plantarum (Linnaeus), 4
Sphagnum moss, use of, 15, 17, 19,
  20, 25, 27
Spiders, red, 42
'Splash,' 71
'Spring Magic,' 97
'Sprite,' 71
'Staghorn Oak,' 75
Standards. See Tree geraniums
'Star of Persia,' 52, 106
'Starlet,' 104
'Stars and Stripes,' 107
Stem rot, 38, 39–40, 131
Stimulants, growth, 28–29
'Strawberry Sundae,' 97
'Summer Cloud,' 52
'Sunset' ('L'Elégante'), 87, 88, 89, 91,
  139
Sweet, Robert, 4
'Sweet William' ('Jeanne'), 106, 145

Tappeiner, John C., 160
Temperature, 16
  in greenhouses, 124–25
'The Blush,' 140
'Tinkerbelle,' 62
'Tiny Tim,' 1, 2, 6, 56, 57
Tobacco budworms, 42
Topiary trees, 137
  for displaying scented-leaved gera-
    niums, 84–85
  of ivy-leaved geraniums, 91, 92
'Toyon,' 33
Transplanting, 20–22
  of Lady Washingtons, 101
  of miniatures, 57–58
  of seedlings, 36
Tree geraniums, 6, 134–37
  fancy-leaved, 69
'Trinket,' 62
True geraniums, 3, 151–56
  drying of, 163
  grown from seed, 154–56
'Turtle's Surprise,' 71

'Variegated Mint-scented Rose,' 75,
  76
'Verona,' 65, 66, 69, 119, 135
'Velma,' 53
Ventilation, 16

Verticillium, 37–39
'Victory Red,' 132
'Village Hill Oak,' 75
'Vin Rouge,' 97
Virus diseases, 41, 130

Waln, Robert, 122
'Waltz Time,' 101
Watering, 14, 19
  in greenhouses, 127–28
'Welcome,' 54
'White Bird's-egg,' 107
White fly, 42
'White Magic,' 133
'White Mesh,' 93
'White Sails,' 99
Wild geraniums. *See* True geraniums
Wilder, Louise Beebe, 156

'Wilhelm Langguth,' 50, 65, 67, 122,
  135
'Will Rogers,' 108
'Willy,' 50
Wintering, 43–46
  of Lady Washingtons, 99–101
  of standards, 135–36
Wittwer, S. H., 29

*Xanthomonas pelargoni,* 39
X-ray treatments to produce mutations, 30

'Yellow Gem,' 65

Zonal geraniums. *See Pelargonium
  hortorum*